DON CHERRY'S
SPORTS HEROES

DON CHERRY'S
SPORTS HEROES

DOUBLEDAY CANADA

Doubleday Canada and colophon are registered trademarks of Penguin Random House Canada Limited

LIBRARY AND ARCHIVES CANADA CATALOGUING IN PUBLICATION

Cherry, Don, 1934– author
    Don Cherry's sports heroes / Don Cherry.

Issued in print electronic formats.
ISBN 978-0-385-68724-9 (hardback).—ISBN 978-0-385-68725-6 (epub)

    1. Cherry, Don, 1934–.   2. Hockey players—Anecdotes.
3. National Hockey League—Anecdotes.   4. Hockey—Anecdotes.
5. Athletes—Anecdotes.   I. Title.

GV848.5 C53 A3 2016   796.962092   C2016-902281-1
                                                 C2016-902282-X

Cover image: Adam d'Oliveira, www.doliveiraphoto.com
Printed and bound in the USA

Published in Canada by Doubleday Canada,
a division of Penguin Random House Canada Limited

www.penguinrandomhouse.ca

10 9 8 7 6 5 4 3 2 1

 Penguin
Random House
DOUBLEDAY CANADA

CONTENTS

DON CHERRY'S
SPORTS HEROES

FOREWORD

Bobby winning another $100 off me by
beating me in the CHL Top Prospects Game in Ottawa.

THERE WAS A NEW COACH WAITING for us when players arrived
at the Boston Bruins' training camp to begin the 1974–75 season.
Don Cherry would be leading what had been the first-place team
in the National Hockey League the season before, no easy task for
someone with relatively little coaching experience.

And yet, he impressed me immediately with his energy and
passion for the game. He had paid his dues in the minors, had
ridden all those buses, and that was something we all respected.
You could sense that he was a player's coach right off the bat,
someone who would be very supportive of the guys in the room.
We learned early on that if we took care of our own end of the ice,
Don was more than happy to let us be creative at the other end.
In the group, we held that philosophy, and it gave us a chance to

win a lot of games. It seemed as if he was born to stand behind the bench of an NHL team. But over time I came to understand that ours would become much more than merely a coach/player relationship. Rather, we would become lifelong friends.

Don was, is and always will be a master storyteller, and this book is wonderful evidence of that fact. As you leaf through these pages, you are going to read many stories that you have probably never previously seen or heard. His extensive connections with so many people in the hockey world allow him to provide us with these anecdotes—stories that may both amuse and challenge the reader at the same time. Make no mistake about it—Don has an opinion and is not afraid to express himself on any number of topics and issues. Of course, his kind of honesty might ruffle some feathers, but I've no doubt you will agree that it all makes for an insightful read.

Don Cherry remains a dear friend, someone I regard as one of the most successful men ever in hockey. A player, coach, analyst and commentator, Don has done it all. His accomplishments both on and off the ice are legendary, his place among the greats assured. And certainly, he continues to be a strong advocate of the game he loves even to this day. With his newest book, Don provides hockey fans the world over with a glimpse into the life and times of "Grapes."

Now . . . just sit back and enjoy!

—Bobby Orr

INTRODUCTION

I AM OFTEN ASKED WHAT I do in my spare time, away from TV and radio. Not too much, to tell you the truth. I don't golf or play sports, I don't fish anymore, and I never go away on vacation.

I watch a lot of TV—mostly sports and the History Channel. What I do most is putter around at home or the cottage. I know it sounds like a humdrum and kind of shallow life. I have travelled so much in my hockey and TV career that home is my refuge.

But there is one thing I look forward to every winter. Going to minor midget games with my son, Tim. It's a joy of my life. Tim rates players in the Greater Toronto Hockey League for the Ontario Hockey League's Central Scouting department. Not too many dads spend so much quality time with their sons.

As I'm writing this, earlier today the Toronto Marlies defeated the Don Mills Flyers 1–0 in overtime in Game Five of an eight-point series to win the GTHL championship. I handed out the medals to the young players. In four or five years, one or two of those players will be NHL-bound and the "experts" will be telling me about them.

I get a kick out of going to the games and seeing the bantams and minor midgets carrying their bags while wearing their shirts and ties. It's the Canadian way. They have respect for the game and themselves. I've heard some dummies say, "Oh, they *make* the kids wear a shirt and tie." I've talked to moms and dads, and they tell me it's a big deal for their kids to go buy their shirts and ties for the season. They want to get dressed up. Some minor midget teams come dressed in full suits. One dad told me his son asked him to carry his bag because the kid didn't want to wrinkle his suit. No other sport does this, and maybe that's why you rarely see a Canadian in the NHL on drugs or in court.

Tim usually picks me up at 8:30 P.M. in our 1997 flareside Ford F-150 truck. It's sort of a community truck — my daughter Cindy, Tim and I all use it for various things as we all live within 100 feet of one another.

Tim and I usually stand down by the glass; let me tell you, some of those rinks are cold. At the end of the second period (they flood between the second and third periods), we go into the boiler room where the Zamboni dumps the snow from the rinks. They usually have a heater to melt the ice, and we try to warm up there.

We often talk about the show where I was the interviewer (for a change) and Tim was the producer. The show was called *Don Cherry's Grapevine*, and it was first shown on CHCH-TV in Hamilton and then on TSN in the 1980s. We had hockey players, baseball players, runners, curlers, boxers, umpires, refs and more. We had everybody. We were never refused an invite; it was the show to be on, as they say.

We only paid $500 and gave the guest a VHS copy of the show. You have to remember that when the show started to air, there was no TSN or Sportsnet and no 24-hour sports radio stations. Not many players had been on TV, so it was a big deal at the time to come on a half-hour talk show. Almost every hockey player who came on the show asked if their mom and dad could come to the taping. It was a big deal for them to have their mom and dad in the audience while they were getting interviewed.

Often in that cold rink we talk about some of the stories that happened on the show. Tim's favourite is the time we had the heavyweight champion of the world, Smokin' Joe Frazier, as a guest. He showed up late and all sweaty, like he had been working out. I'll tell you the full story in Smokin' Joe's chapter.

One time, at the end of the second period of a minor midget game, while warming up in the boiler room as usual, we started talking about the great stories of Joe Frazier and Bobby Orr, the Rocket, MLB umpire Ron Luciano and some of the other great guests we had on the show.

Tim said, "Dad, why don't we do a book on the show? We could tell how the show got started—the inside stuff that happened behind the scenes." As Tim was the producer, wrote the questions and booked the guests—with help from his mother, Rose—he remembered most of what went on. I thought it was a great idea.

So in the cold boiler room, we decided to do the book. I hope you enjoy the stories.

—Don Cherry

GERRY PATTERSON

On the set of the *Grapevine* show with my good friend
and one-time agent, Gerry Patterson. He was a big help when
I first started in television and was a really great guy.

GERRY PATTERSON, SHOWDOWN AND BOXES TO SUCCESS

ONE OF THE EXECUTIVE PRODUCERS OF the *Don Cherry's
Grapevine* show was my good friend and agent, Gerry Patterson.
Gerry was an agent for Jean Béliveau, Ken Dryden and other successful athletes. I first met Gerry on the set of a television feature
called "Showdown."

Before I get into telling you about Gerry, I want to tell you about
"Showdown," which was a hugely successful and very controversial feature of *Hockey Night in Canada*. The show was taped back
in the late 1970s and early '80s in a small neighbourhood rink just
north of Toronto. It was kind of the start of today's skills competition and three-on-three tournament at the NHL All-Star Game.

Teams were made up of four players and a goalie. I remember one team had Gilbert Perreault, Darryl Sittler, Jean Ratelle and Steve Shutt, so you can see these were, at the time, the top NHL stars.

They would hold a series of competitions, for different amounts of points, and the winning team would move on to the next round. It was a round-robin tournament, so each week different groups of NHL stars would compete against each other until someone was crowned a winner.

Segments ran between the second and third period on *Hockey Night in Canada*. No one who worked on the show ever let it be known who won, so the winners would be a surprise to the audience.

It got huge ratings. Some people would tune in to the game just to watch "Showdown," just like they do today for "Coach's Corner." When kids would play street hockey, they didn't say, "Let's play hockey," they'd say, "Let's play 'Showdown.'"

The CBC and the National Hockey League Players' Association put it on, and it was very controversial, especially in Toronto. The NHL wasn't too happy with the whole thing, and the owner of the Maple Leafs, Harold Ballard, went to war with Leafs captain Darryl Sittler over it.

Ballard forbade Sittler, and Leaf players Lanny McDonald, Mike Palmateer and Börje Salming, from playing in the 1979 "Showdown" series because Salming broke his finger playing in the competition one year.

Sittler defied Harold's warning and risked his wrath. Things got worse between Ballard and Sittler. I was coaching Colorado at the time, and we called the Leafs GM, Punch Imlach, to see if we could trade for Sittler. They couldn't move Sittler because he had a no-trade clause in his contract. Then we were told we could have Lanny McDonald and Joel Quenneville for Pat Hickey and Wilf Paiement. So we made the trade.

Just a reminder that Joel went on to win three Stanley Cups as the coach of the Hawks. One of the Hawks' assistant coaches is

Mike Kitchen, who also played in Colorado with Joel. They both must have learned from a good coach they played for.

Leafs fans loved Lanny, and when the news got out about the trade, the city of Toronto went nuts. Sittler was so angry that he ripped his captain's C off his Leafs sweater.

An announcer on *Hockey Night in Canada* said he didn't blame Darryl for ripping the C off his sweater. Ballard was so upset at the announcer that he told *Hockey Night in Canada* to get their cameras out of the Gardens if that announcer was in the building. So the announcer had to do games from the Montreal Forum for the rest of his career.

So you can see that "Showdown" caused a lot controversy, but boy did the audience love it.

Gerry Patterson was one of the promoters and producers of "Showdown." For a couple of years, I worked on the show as a so-called interviewer. I'd interview players between competitions and ask some questions. In the last year of the show, the summer of 1980, I was having a tough time. I had just been fired from Colorado and I was getting the feeling that I was blackballed. I was starting to think that I wasn't going to get another coaching offer.

In two years, I had gone to war with two GMs, Boston's Harry Sinden and Colorado's Ray Miron. The NHL was an old boys' club, and the word was getting around that I was hard to deal with. Can you imagine that?

Ralph Mellanby, the executive producer of *Hockey Night in Canada* as well as "Showdown," hired me to do some games for *Hockey Night in Canada*. You must realize that, back in those days, *Hockey Night in Canada* paid next to nothing. They felt it was a privilege to work for them. I have to admit, I was getting famous, but I was still poor.

I was scratching around, doing the odd banquet tour and getting by, as they say. Hey, I was happy just to have a job.

From the show, Gerry and I became friends, and soon he became my agent. I remember like it was yesterday. He said, "Grapes, I'm going to draw you some boxes and you're going to be a success on television. From there, you're going to become very successful."

I thought he was nuts, but I went along with him. I had nothing to lose.

Gerry got a piece of paper and he drew the boxes to my so-called successful career. He was the most positive guy I have ever met. He kept saying, "Grapes, you have to believe."

I said to Gerry, "I believe. I believe." I will admit, in my heart I said I believed, but in my head, I didn't believe.

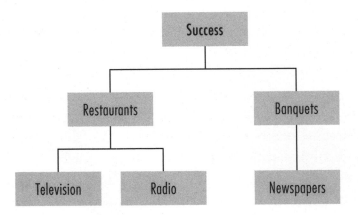

These were the boxes Gerry drew—the blueprint for my success. Gerry started out helping me fill in these boxes.

Gerry was one of Ralph Mellanby's best friends. Not only was Ralph executive producer of *Hockey Night in Canada,* but he was the head of broadcasting for the Olympic Games and won numerous awards all over the world for his producing skills. I'm convinced that Gerry's friendship with Ralph was one of the reasons Ralph kept me on *Hockey Night in Canada.*

Gerry and Ralph came up with a plan to do a television show where I would interview sports heroes. They would call it *Don Cherry's Grapevine,* a little play on my nickname, Grapes.

At first, I didn't want to do it. I had never really interviewed anyone before—I had just reacted to questions from Dave Hodge on "Coach's Corner"—but Gerry insisted that if we were going to fill in those boxes he had drawn, we needed to do this show.

CHCH, Channel 11 in Hamilton, Ontario, was willing to take a chance. Remember, there were no 24-hour sports stations on television or radio, so doing an all-sports interview show in prime time was a big risk. I'm sure Ralph's reputation was the main reason that CHCH agreed to do the show.

They hired two comedians, Bill Lynn and Jimmy Loftus, to help out, and singer John Allan Cameron to do a song in the middle of the show. The reason they hired these guys was because Ralph and Gerry needed a backup plan if I couldn't pull it off. I struggled mightily at the start, but I stuck it out. So now I had one boxed filled—television.

For the next box to be checked, Gerry wanted me to write a column in a newspaper. He contacted a young fellow who worked for the *Vancouver Sun*. He asked about me writing a column once a week.

Well, in for a penny, in for a pound, and away I go, writing a sports column. I was made fun of by the other newspaper guys.

I remember one guy saying, "What's Grapes going to write about, Schmautzy all the time?" (Bobby Schmautz was one of my favourite players. He played for me in Rochester, Boston and Colorado, and ended his career in Vancouver. I consider him one of my good friends.)

I used to send my column to a young fellow named Paul Chapman and he would put it in the *Sun*. I did this the whole winter. One day, the *Sun* took a poll on who had the best column in the newspaper, and 75 percent voted for me. Like Ali said, "It's not bragging if you can back it up."

I did it for a couple of years, and I enjoyed it; another box filled.

The next box to fill was radio. Again, at this time there was no 24-hour sports television or radio, so doing a radio program all about sports was kind of a long shot.

Gerry had the idea of only doing a short, two- or three-minute program, covering one topic and telling stories. Gerry had the guts of a burglar. He went to Bridgestone Tire and said, "Don Cherry is going to do a radio program on CFRB, and it's going to be a great success. If you want to be part of it, we need to you come up with some dough."

They agreed to be the sponsors. Gerry then went to Prior Smith at CFRB and said, "Don Cherry wants to do a radio show for your station."

Prior said, "Oh yeah is that right? Well, there's a line 50-feet long of people who want to do a radio show. What makes you think you'd get one?"

Gerry then handed him a cheque for $100,000. Prior brought on my good friend Brian Williams from CBC Sports as co-host and the show took off from there. *Don Cherry's Grapeline* has been on the air for over 30 years, is on over 100 stations, and has over a million weekly listeners. Another box filled in by Gerry.

Now things were going well for me. Gerry had filled out three boxes on the diagram, and now it was time to fill in another: banquets.

I don't want to say we didn't have any money, but *Hockey Night in Canada* was still not paying a lot, and the newspaper column and radio show were helping out moneywise. But you have to remember, this was in the mid-'80s—I had a new house, the first time Rose had ever moved into a new house, and interest rates were running around 21.5 percent. So any money coming in helped.

Gerry started booking banquets for me. He'd pick me up and drive me to the events. We'd have some great talks on the way to the banquets. On the way to a banquet in Goderich, Ontario, Gerry taught me a lesson that I still abide by to this day.

I had written a speech about my thoughts on the meaning of life and how to become a successful coach and stuff. On the way to Goderich, I practised my speech, and when I was done, I asked Gerry what he thought.

I had worked a week on it and thought it was Shakespeare quality. Gerry turned to me and said, "Horseshit! Grapes, all they want is the Don Cherry on 'Coach's Corner.' They want to hear stories about Bobby Orr, Eddie Shore. Not hear your philosophy of life."

I realized Gerry was right. From then on, when I did a banquet—funny thing is, when I didn't get paid much to do banquets, I did a ton, and now that I can get some good dough to do banquets, I don't do any—I'd tell a few jokes and tell stories about the Bruins, Bobby Orr and *Hockey Night in Canada*.

I also keep it short. Tim tells me the secret to my success is brevity. Tell funny stories, keep it short and leave them wanting more. Another box filled in by Gerry.

As the years went by, the *Grapevine* show became very successful. We had great audience numbers and all the NHL stars wanted to be on the show.

The show was set in an English pub–like setting, so in 1984 Gerry said, "It's time to open up a real bar called the Grapevine."

All I knew about restaurants was how to order food in them. Gerry insisted that this was the next step in becoming successful. So Gerry and I went all over the Greater Toronto Area, looking at failed restaurants. I wanted a bar or restaurant like the ones I went to in Boston. The rent in Toronto was crazy and I couldn't see how you could make any money.

There was nothing in Toronto to be found, and then one day someone said, "Why not look in Hamilton, Ontario? It's a blue-collar steel town and they all like 'Coach's Corner.'"

So Gerry and I set off again in his old brown Mercedes, this time to Hamilton, and the first place we looked at was perfect. It was on the corner of Main and Walnut in downtown Hamilton. It was just what I was looking for—old barn wood, a large wrap-around bar with lots of character, big booths, which I loved, and a big dance floor.

I have to say, it was in bad shape. I don't know what had happened, but it looked like the customers got up and ran out of the place before it closed for good. On the tables there were still bowls of soup with the spoons in them that had been there for a year. It was kind of gross.

It was dirty, but being in bars for most of my hockey career, I knew it had potential. I loved it, but unfortunately Gerry didn't and wanted no part of it, and this is where we started to drift apart.

A guy named Rick Scully, who had lots of experience in the restaurant business, became my partner. Rick and I renovated the place, put in lots of great hockey pictures and televisions to watch the game, and it was a smashing success. People were lined up around the block to get in. It became a big-time dance bar. Gerry filled in the last box.

Soon, Gerry decided to take the *Grapevine* television show out of the CHCH studios and shoot it live in the bar. After about five years of shooting in the bar, the show got too expensive to do. Plus, I would do two and sometimes three shows a night, and it was getting to be too much. We ended the show and Gerry and I drifted further apart.

Gerry had said I had to believe that if we filled in all the boxes he drew, I would be a success. Like I said, at the time I wanted to believe him, but I had my doubts.

Gerry has been gone some 10 years now. He was walking his dog in the middle of winter and someone needed help shovelling their driveway. Wouldn't you know, Gerry died helping somebody.

I better be careful here. I can hear Gerry saying, "Don't get philosophical, just tell some funny stories."

WAYNE GRETZKY

Wayne was only 21 years old when he came on the *Grapevine*.
Hard to believe all the records Wayne would set in the following 15 years.

THE GREAT SALESMAN AND MOTIVATOR

THERE HAS NEVER BEEN A GUY in any sport who could sell his game like Wayne Gretzky. Never does he turn down an interview and he is always positive.

I remember when I was coaching the Colorado Rockies in 1979–80 and we were playing the Oilers. I arrived at McNichols Sports Arena around 5 P.M., and as I was walking along the hall, here comes Gretzky in his underwear, sweater and flip-flops, heading to do a live interview on a local station to help the Rockies organization. He did it to help sell the game in Denver and get a good crowd that night. All those interviews helped him become pretty comfortable in front of the camera.

Wayne was the guest on the first *Don Cherry's Grapevine* to air.

We shot the show on July 4, 1982, and it aired two months later. Hard to believe he was only 21 years old.

I started out by teasing Wayne, saying he looked like Eddie Haskell from *Leave It to Beaver* and asking him how he felt when he nailed a kid with a golf ball in the Canadian Open. But Wayne was ready for me.

WAYNE: I got a question for you.

DON: All right, go ahead.

WAYNE: I've been following your career. I see you have your own TV show now, and that's great. You do a great job on *Hockey Night in Canada*. You fancy yourself as a good dresser. But I want you to know: I'm in the top 10 best-dressed males in America and you're not.

DON: Ha, fame is fleeting.

You could see that, even at only 21 years old, Wayne had the art of being interviewed down to a T. He never said anything controversial, smooth as silk, always said the right things. You'd never catch him.

Now fast-forward 20 years to the Olympics, and Wayne was the executive director of the Canadian men's hockey team. The only interview where he appeared to let his guard down was at these Olympics. He went wild about how Canada was getting stiffed in the early games.

It was after a 3–3 tie with the Czechs. The team's record was 1–1–1 and the media was getting on Team Canada. Theo Fleury got mixed up with Czech goalie Dominik Hašek and Czech defenceman Roman Hamrlík cross-checked Fleury in the back, a real good shot. No penalties. In the press conference, a seething Wayne went on to say,

I know the whole world wants us to lose except Canada and Canadian fans. We respect every team we play. We don't dislike them. Maybe when we start to dislike them, we play better. I don't think we dislike these countries as much as they hate us, and that's a fact. They don't like us. They want to see us fail. They love beating us. And we've got to get the same feeling toward them . . . Am I hot? Yes, I'm hot. I'm tired of people taking shots at Canadian hockey. . . . When we do it, we're hooligans. And when Europeans do it, it's OK. When a Czech does it, it's OK. I don't understand it. There was a spear and a cross-check on the same play. If it was a Canadian player who did it, it would be a big story.

It worked. He rallied the troops, got the attention of the refs, and we won. He's always in control in an interview.

WAYNE AND WALTER GRETZKY

IF I GET ASKED ONE QUESTION over and over, it's "When should I start my kid skating?" I always like to know how young the superstars were when they started to skate.

DON: When did you start skating?

WAYNE: Let's see . . . 19 years ago, so I started at two, so 21 years, that's almost as long as Gordie Howe has played.

When you read about young Wayne, the topic of the backyard rink his dad, Walter, built always comes up. They called it "Wally's Coliseum," and soon all the neighbourhood kids would come around and play.

We had Walter on the show a year after Wayne's show (why we didn't have both of them on at the same time, I'll never figure out; sometimes you just blank—I'll blame Gerry and Tim on this one), and he told us about the famous rink.

DON: So why did you build the rink in the backyard?

WALTER: Self-preservation. One of the first times I took Wayne to the outdoor rink at the park, it had to have been about 15 below that night. I said, "Come on, Wayne, let's go," and he said, "No, just a few more minutes, Dad." Now everybody is gone, the lights are turned off and I'm still sitting in the car, that's running, but I'm still frozen. When we got home, I said, "Well, Phyllis, from now on I'm putting a rink in the backyard."

DON: Now, I have to ask you, and you're not bragging, but at what age could you tell he had a special gift?

WALTER: I like to answer that in two ways. As far as a minor hockey player, at four or five years old you could see he had that special gift you're talking about and [that] he would be exceptional in minor hockey. As you know yourself, better than I do, you don't know if someone is going to be a professional player till they are 16 or 17 years old, or older, because things can change.

DON: I once read something that said you taught Wayne anticipation. I always thought you had hockey anticipation or not, but you say no, it can be taught, and you taught Wayne to anticipate.

WALTER: I really believe it can be taught. If you're a small player, you have to be able to do something a big player can't, and the one thing everybody can do is think. I tried to get Wayne and the rest of the kids to think out on the ice, so I told them that anticipation is just out-thinking the other player, and to me it's so simple. An example is if you stand at the blue line and fire the puck around the boards—I always show them that a lot of kids will follow the puck all the way into the corner, behind the net to the other corner. Well, I just showed them if you fire the puck around the boards, don't chase the puck. Just go where the puck's going to be.

DON: No wonder I spent all those years in the minors. I was chasing the puck all the time. Now I got to ask ya, when Wayne was young, he wore those white gloves and caught a lot of flak because of it. Tell how he got those gloves.

WALTER: Whoo, let me tell you, that was not intentional. It was one of those days. It was the first practice of the year, and Wayne didn't have any gloves that fit him, and I was working late that night and we rushed over to the sporting-goods store, and the owner was a good friend of ours. I said, "We need a pair of gloves as fast as you can. We only have 20 minutes to get him on the rink and on the ice." He said, "I have just the pair for ya." He reached up and took down these white gloves and I said, "Put them right back, I don't want any part of them." The owner said, "Just let him try them on." Wayne said, "They look nice, Dad." So he put them on. They were very flexible, and I like flexible equipment for kids. Wayne liked them, so we took them and that's how the white gloves started.

DON: Now, everybody wants to know about tucking the sweater in. Where did that come from. Did you teach him that?

WALTER: No. Again, it was something that he had to do because he was so small. He was six years old, playing with 10-year-olds, and the sweater hung down to his ankles, so I told him just to tuck it in the corner of his pants. He got used to it and has done it ever since.

* * *

I had met Walter at a charity event a few months before we interviewed Wayne, and he was concerned about his son.

DON: Now, I talked to your dad, and he's a little worried that you are doing too many events during the summer and not getting enough downtime.

WAYNE: Sooner or later, it's going to catch up. It's not going to bother me next season. I was busier last summer than I was this summer. This summer, I decided to take more time off. It's been pretty hectic, but I have some time off.

DON: Well, ya know I had the number one guy in Bobby Orr. It got to the point they were bothering him in warm-up. They were grabbing him five minutes before the game. It got to the point, when he got to a town, he'd go to his room and we'd never see him till before game time. You gotta watch that.

WAYNE: Someday it might lead up to that for me. The demand for his [Bobby's] time is so hectic. Everybody knew Bobby Orr from coast to coast and in the U.S. because he played for Boston. Right now, it's not as tough for me as it was for him. Hopefully, it won't get as bad for me as it was for him that they bothered him the day of the game. Ya know, when your hockey starts sliding, they are not going to bother you.

Like I said off the top, Wayne kept up selling the game. There is no doubt in my mind that the reason Anaheim and San Jose are in the NHL is because of the way Wayne sold the game when he was traded to the Los Angeles Kings.

THE ESPOSITO SYNDROME AND FIGHTING

IN 1981–82, THE SEASON THAT HAD just ended when Wayne came on the *Grapevine*, he scored 92 goals and had 212 points, and expectations were bound to be high going into the next season. The first year I coached in Boston, Phil Esposito was coming off a 77-goal season (68 in the regular season and 9 in the playoffs). The next season, I saw the pressure that was on Phil to get back to 77 goals. The pressure was on him all year.

> **DON:** You got 92 goals last year. [A few years before I went to coach Boston,] Phil got 76 goals. The next year, he got 66 goals, still All-World, but the media headlines said, ESPOSITO'S BAD YEAR. So you got to get 90 next year or else.

> **WAYNE:** I guess the pressure's on. I always said you only do as well as your team does. We've proved that the last three years. As the team climbed, I climbed as an individual, and so did everybody else. For next season, if we play as well as we did last season, then I have the opportunity to play as well as an individual as I did last season. Because you're only as strong as your team, and every player that plays a team sport knows that. You have to use your teammates to your advantage.

So how did Wayne do that next year? Well, he didn't hit 90 goals but he still got 71 goals and 196 points. Not too bad. The Oilers went to their first Stanley Cup final, but lost to the Islanders in four straight games. The year after that, the Oilers dynasty started, with them winning five out of the next seven Stanley Cups.

* * *

DON: If you could change any rule, what would you change?

WAYNE: Hmm, if I can change any rule, I would like to take out the blue line—forget taking out the red line. Ya know, when I start talking about changing rules, I have to be careful. All of a sudden people start saying, "Oh, he's being a baby and starting to cry about the rules." But if there is one thing I think they should change—everybody loves the body contact that is in professional hockey, and I think it's great. But when guys start trying to deliberately hurt someone with a hockey stick, there should be severe penalties. The league is rough and it's going to get rougher, but the intentional hurting of a player has to stop.

DON: OK then, what do you think about fighting? In pro hockey.

WAYNE: It goes along with what I just said: if you stop the fighting, there's going to be more spearing and more slashing, and that's the stuff we have to stop. You know, I can take a punch from anyone—well, maybe not [teammate Dave] Semenko.

DON: Oh, he'd never hit you. You're worth 200 grand to him. Tell us about Semenko.

WAYNE: He's not going anywhere if I have anything to say about it. He's tremendous, and he's one of my favourites. What I like about David, he's far and away the strongest and toughest man that I've ever seen play the game of hockey [in terms] of dropping the gloves and fighting. But he doesn't do that unless he feels he needs to.

DON: Having him just on the bench is intimidating. I remember coaching against him, and if somebody runs at you, let's be honest, he goes out and gives them a stare.

WAYNE: Sometimes he does more than stare. But you notice he played regular most of the year, but some games he didn't, but when I come off the ice I always sit beside him.

DON: But that's what the tough guys are for, so no one runs around and takes advantage of the stars.

WAYNE: I couldn't take a slash or a spear from a stick. I think fighting has to stay, there's nothing wrong with it. Dropping the gloves and having a one-on-one, it doesn't hurt hockey and people like to see the odd fight. In many ways, it's safer. Remember, we carry a lethal weapon. And you have to remember that.

DON: You try and tell people that and they hear the word *fighting* and they automatically think it's wrong. No, we're not talking about kids, we're talking about men.

WAYNE: I'm being honest. I'd play in the NHL and see the fighting which goes on, then play in Czechoslovakia, Russia, Finland or Sweden. Those guys, that's what you call rough hockey. I'm more nervous playing the Czechs than playing Philly in Philly.

At one point after Wayne retired, he said something along the line that fighting should be taken out of the game, but he came to his senses and echoed what he said in a 2007 article in Sun Media:

*"I don't love fighting, it's not something I tell my players to do, and
it's not something I would do. But as stupid as it sounds, it probably
prevents a lot of stick infractions.*

*"The unique thing about our sport is that we play with hockey
sticks that potentially can be used as weapons. This is a game that
is very emotional and guys are only human. Fighting gives them
an outlet to release (energy and frustrations) instead of slashing,
cross-checking and high-sticking.*

*"You almost never see a tough guy grab a small skilled guy and
start (punching) either. There is still a code."*

Gretzky said his stance has softened a bit with time.

"I've gone back and forth over the years," he said.

When Wayne was in his heyday in Edmonton, some people
thought there was a "You can't hit Gretzky" rule. That was because
of the presence of Dave Semenko and then Marty McSorley. If
you hit Wayne or were bugging him, Semenko or McSorley would
tell you once to stop, and the next time you'd get it. When Wayne
was traded to LA, he wanted Marty to go with him and it wasn't for
his goal scoring.

When Steve Yzerman had six 100-point seasons in a row, he had
Bob Probert and Joey Kocur to watch out for him. When Brett
Hull scored 72 goals, he had a tough guy named Kelly Chase to
watch out for him. The Islanders' Mike Bossy had Clark Gillies
and Bobby Nystrom to look out for him. Jean Béliveau was pro-
tected by John Ferguson.

On pretty much any team, if you fooled around with a star,
you'd have to pay a dear price. But once the instigator rule was put
in by the NHL (Gil Stein was running the league then) it became
open season on the stars.

I saw a lot of things when Wayne was on the ice. I saw him score
five goals in one game to set a record of 50 goals in 39 games. A
record never to be broken.

I've seen him score a beauty overtime goal against Calgary. I saw him score a goal from behind the net in Game 7 to beat the Toronto Maple Leafs and put LA in the Stanley Cup final.

I saw him score the goal that broke Gordie Howe's all-time scoring record. But on January 3, 1981, I saw something that I never thought I'd see.

DON: I want to get into right now . . . I was in Edmonton last year, you were playing Toronto, the hardest check I ever saw in my life, was by Bill McCreary (Jr.) on you at the blue line. Tell me about it.

WAYNE: Well, unfortunately, I had my head down, which is a no-no in hockey. To my defence, I don't think it was all my fault. First of all, we were playing against a team with three minutes left in the game and we were winning by a big score. The puck came out of our zone and I looked over and saw my winger, and I thought I had a two-on-one. Now, if he was a defenceman, he would have backed up, but he was a forward and forwards can't play defence, so he charged me and nailed me.

DON: I thought you were dead.

WAYNE: I thought I was too.

LOST INVITATION

I WAS SURPRISED IN THE EARLY spring of 1988 that Rose and I got an invitation to Wayne and Janet's wedding in Edmonton.

The invitation was a work of art. Rose wanted to make sure we kept it.

So we go to the wedding that July. Let me tell you, if Canada ever had a Royal Wedding, this was it. The weather was perfect. Wayne was decked out in a beauty tux and Janet had an unbelievable wedding dress. Janet was gorgeous. The wedding cake had to be four feet tall.

At the reception, we first sat at the back with Kirk Muller, Gus Badali (Wayne's one-time agent) and some other hockey players. We were having a grand time, laughing and telling stories.

Then someone asked me to move tables and go sit with a movie star, Fred Dryer (I remember when the soup came he picked it up and drank it straight out of the bowl)—he starred in a show called *Hunter*—and some other owners I didn't know.

They were nice, but I could hear Kirk laughing and having a great time with all the players. I had to make small talk with these people I didn't know, wishing I was back having a few beers with Gus and Kirk.

Anyway, when we got home, Rose said, "Don't lose that invitation. I want to develop the pictures we took at the wedding and put it in my scrapbook."

So I put it in one of my many, many old books to keep it safe and to make sure it didn't get accidently bent.

A few weeks later, Rose got the pictures developed and asked me to get the invitation. I couldn't remember what book I put it in, and to this day the invitation is still missing.

Rose was pretty upset and said that she should have known better than to let me take care of it. I give a lot of my old books away for charity book sales—I bet someone bought a book on Lord Nelson at a charity book sale and found an invitation to Wayne and Janet Greztky's wedding stuck between the pages.

When I interviewed the Rocket in 1984 I asked him about Wayne Gretzky. The Rocket said, "He's a natural and he's hard to beat. If he doesn't get any injuries he will set all new records in the league." The Rocket sure called that one.

I remember somebody said to Wayne, "Oh, you scored all those points and goals when hockey was played wide open."

Wayne had the greatest answer when he looked at the guy and said, "I didn't see anybody else doing it."

JOE FRAZIER

It was a great honour to have heavyweight champion
of the world Smokin' Joe Frazier on the show.

THE ORIGINAL ROCKY

I LOVE WATCHING HOCKEY, BUT I have to say boxing is a close second. I used to go to all the closed-circuit telecasts of fights, starting when I was in my 20s.

In our first year of the *Grapevine* show, Ralph Mellanby told me Smokin' Joe Frazier was going to be one of our first guests. Like I mentioned at the start of the book, the show was supposed to start taping at 7 P.M. The time was approaching and Joe and the limo were nowhere to be found. There were no cell phones back then, so we had no idea what was going on.

Suddenly, Joe burst in all sweaty, his shirt dirty. The limo had gotten a flat tire driving Joe from the Toronto airport to the Hamilton studio. The limo driver was an older gentleman, and he said, "I can't change a tire."

Joe said, "Don't worry about it, I've changed lots of tires," and he took off his coat and rolled up his sleeves, got the jack out of the trunk and changed the tire.

I wonder if anybody driving by recognized the heavyweight champion of the world, Smokin' Joe Frazier, changing a tire on a limo on the side of the QEW.

Joe wasn't a really tall man. He was around six feet, but he was stocky. Even in his street clothes, you could see he was a powerful guy. When he showed up for the taping of the show, it was just Joe. I thought he'd have an entourage with him, but he just flew in from Philly by himself.

This was one of my first shows, and I can tell you I was pretty excited and nervous to interview the heavyweight champion of the world.

> **DON:** You have to forgive me if I'm a little nervous here; you're one of my heroes. So let's start off the bat: *Rocky* was kind of taken from your life. You worked in the slaughterhouse, and that helped you build up strength.

> **SMOKIN' JOE:** Yes, I worked in a slaughterhouse from about '62 to '64. I ran the streets of Philadelphia and went to the gym. It's crazy. I used to go to the gym so late at night, the owner gave me a key. Everybody was gone, everybody went home. My hours at the slaughterhouse was 4 A.M. and I'd work to 6 P.M., and then I'd go to the gym, and after the gym I'd go to the park and run.

> **DON:** That's dedication. You worked at the slaughterhouse and you slaughtered a lot of guys. Now, is it true you tried out for a role in one of the *Rocky* films? You were supposed to play the Mr. T. role, and you didn't get it. What happened?

SMOKIN' JOE: Well, the *Rocky* movies were built around a former champion: myself. I really worked in a slaughter-house. I used to punch the sides of beef. Stallone couldn't cut a side of beef with a saw. I'd take that side of beef apart.

DON: Just like you did to Ali in the Garden.

SMOKIN' JOE: Ya know, my job is my job, no matter what it be. I learned to always do my job well. Ya know, the time I worked at the slaughterhouse—it was a good job. It was a good living for my family.

DON: It was an honest job.

SMOKIN' JOE: Yes, I had to make a living for my family. At the time, I wasn't fighting as much as I should because I was growing up as a young man with a young family and I had to take care of them.

DON: As a young boy, I remember listening to Foster Hewitt on the radio, and I knew I wanted to be a hockey player. Did you know you wanted to be a fighter at a young age?

SMOKIN' JOE: It's crazy. I tried to play baseball.

DON: I heard you were a catcher?

SMOKIN' JOE: No! You couldn't get me behind the plate. I'd play any position, but not behind that bat. I couldn't see the ball coming anyway. So I played baseball for a while when I lived in the South. But it's crazy—a man, a person, is born to be. Do you know what I mean?

DON: Fate.

SMOKIN' JOE: Yeah, he's to be what he's to be. When I was a young kid, my daddy and my uncle would point to me and say, "See that boy there? He's going to be another Joe Louis." I kept hearing that in my head. In the South, they didn't have no facilities, so I got a burlap sack and I stuffed it with cloth and hung it on the tree, and that would be my punching bag.

THE GOLDEN AGE OF THE HEAVYWEIGHTS AND ALI

SMOKIN' JOE'S STYLE WAS KIND OF like Iron Mike Tyson's—or, I should say, Mike Tyson's style was like Joe Frazier's. Both of them had the style of my favourite boxer of all time, the Manassa Mauler, Jack Dempsey. Not a step back; hunched over, bobbing and weaving; and every punch had bad intentions.

One time during one of the playoff series between my Bruins and the Montreal Canadiens, a Boston reporter said that the Canadiens were like Muhammad Ali and the Bruins were like Smokin' Joe Frazier. He was right. My Bruins played like Joe fought. Always moving forward, always pounding away at the other team's defence. We played in a frenzy and just wanted to wear you down.

Smokin' Joe never took a step backwards, and I never liked it when we went backwards with the puck. I wanted my forwards to dump the puck in on the fly and go after the defence. Oilers defenceman Kevin Lowe told me one day how he hated playing the Bruins in the Garden. He said that the wingers used to play "leansies" with the puck against the boards and would just hammer him. He said he got to know the people sitting in the first row of the Garden well.

When Joe was in his heyday in the late '60s and early '70s, it was the golden age of the heavyweights. Ali had just been stripped of his title, and Frazier, Jimmy Ellis, George Foreman, Oscar Bonavena, Jerry Quarry and Canada's George Chuvalo were all looking to take the heavyweight belt. Back then, all those guys were household names. Today, I couldn't name two heavyweights.

Smokin' Joe became heavyweight champ on February 16, 1970, at Madison Square Garden. I remember going to the Rochester War Memorial to see the fight on closed-circuit TV.

He was fighting Jimmy Ellis for the undisputed heavyweight title. The oddsmakers in Las Vegas had Smokin' Joe as the favourite, but more than half the writers at the weigh-in in New York said Ellis was going to win. Right from the start, Joe just kept coming. He never took a step back. Ellis was the quicker puncher, but Joe just kept coming, pounding Ellis's body. I guess Joe was following the old boxing saying, "Kill the body and the head will die."

By the second round, you could tell the body shots were taking their toll and Ellis was slowing down. When Smokin' Joe got in close, Ellis was starting to hold Joe, and Joe started to give him some head-butts to stop him from holding. Towards the end of the second round, Ellis was against the ropes and Smokin' Joe was just teeing off on his ribs. Howard Cosell was calling the fight and he kept saying "Frazier the pursuer" as Joe stalked Ellis.

In the third round, as Cosell would go on to say, "A stupendous left hook by Frazier changed the course of the fight. Joe Frazier in utter dominance now." Joe's left hook caught Ellis right on the button, and he was in trouble the whole round. How Ellis finished that third round, I'll never know.

In the fourth round, Smokin' Joe reminded me of a lumberjack chopping down a tree. He just kept pounding the body until, with less than a minute to go, Ellis just collapsed from all those body shots. He got up, and then, with around 11 seconds left in the round, a huge left hook to the jaw put Ellis down again. He got up, but Ellis's trainer, Angelo Dundee, stopped the fight. Joe became the undisputed heavyweight champion of the world.

Back then, no title on earth held as much stature as undisputed heavyweight champion of the world.

> **DON:** Now, tell us about the responsibility of a heavyweight champion. Ya know, if the heavyweights are going good, then boxing is going good. It seems to rest on your shoulders.

> **SMOKIN' JOE:** Well, the responsibility of being heavyweight champ is the same to be an athlete like yourself. You have to take pride in it; nobody should have to tell you what you have to do, or when to do it. Most of my time is spent in the gym with my boys and my nephews. These guys don't have any trouble getting up early and going running in the park in the morning, or showing up at the gym at the right time, ready to work. No shortcut on the work; they want to be the best they can be. That relates to a good athlete and a good champ or good man.

When you talk about Joe Frazier, you always have to talk about Ali. They had three of the greatest fights of all time. The first one was on March 8, 1971, in Madison Square Garden. It was a brutal fight, and Smokin' Joe knocked Ali down late in the fight. It went all 15 rounds and Smokin' Joe won by a unanimous decision. Both men ended up in the hospital after the fight. They met again in New York three years later.

When there is a big fight nowadays, there is always this phony kind of trash talk or pushing and shoving at the weigh-in to try to promote the fight. That stuff really didn't happen until Ali and Frazier went on television with Howard Cosell.

DON: You know, when you and Ali were going at it at the press conferences and the weigh-ins, was that staged? Ya know, when you two were trying to get each other?

SMOKIN' JOE: Before he got his boxing licence back, a lot of it was staged. We had a workout together at a small PAL [Police Athletic League] gym in Philadelphia, and there was such a crowd we'd block up traffic for miles. Now, those things were staged. But it got to the point, as time went by, he got his boxing licence and mouth licence back, and then he changed. So when he changed, I saw a difference in the man that I used to know as being an OK guy to acting the way he did. So I changed too.

DON: You could tell for a while that you were going along with it, but with the Cosell thing, you said, "You're not going to make a fool of me anymore."

SMOKIN' JOE: Right.

This is what happened. To promote their rematch on January 23, 1974, famed sports announcer Howard Cosell was shooting a television show with Ali and Frazier in the ABC Sports studio, talking about their first fight. They showed each round of the first fight, and both Ali and Frazier would talk about what was going on in the fight.

Cosell did this a few times with different fights, and it was always a great show to watch. As the show went on, Ali was making fun of Joe and Joe was getting mad. As they went to the final commercial break, you could tell Joe was agitated. They came back from the commercial and started to show the 10th round. Joe said something about Ali going to the hospital after the fight.

Ali seemed to get mad and said, "Don't bring up the hospital . . . that shows how dumb you are, bringing up the hospital."

They were talking over each other about the hospital and Cosell was trying to get them to talk about the fight. They went from joking to not joking in a real hurry.

Ali said, "That shows how ignorant you are, talking about the hospital."

Joe got up from his seat and stood over Ali and said, "Why do you think I'm ignorant?"

Ali said, "Sit down, Joe. Sit down, Joe."

Joe kept saying, "Why do you think I'm ignorant?"

This is when you could tell it was getting real. One of Ali's entourage grabbed Joe by the arm and Joe looked at him, ready to drill him, and said, "You want some too?"

Ali stood up and grabbed Joe. They wrestled for a minute. At first, Cosell thought it was a put-on. As they started going at it, Cosell said very calmly, "Well, they're having a scene, as you can see. It's hard to tell if it's clowning or real between the two fighters. This kind of thing has been going on all along in terms of promotion of the fight."

Then Cosell started to get a little panicky. "This time, it seems to be for real, because Joe Frazier is really angry. Muhammad called him ignorant and he's really angry. I'd say this one isn't clowning at all."

The other reason I think it was for real was that Joe left the set. No way he'd leave and let Ali run his mouth without him there if he wasn't steaming mad. The New York State Athletic Commission fined both men $5,000 for their actions and went on to say if one of them got hurt, just days before the fight, it would have cost the city and the promoters millions of dollars.

Joe went on to lose that second fight, Ali getting the unanimous decision. That set up the rubber match, the Thrilla in Manila— some say the greatest heavyweight fight of all time. Ali was calling

Joe a gorilla at all the press conferences. Joe lost when his corner stopped the fight in the 14th round.

I read that one of the reasons Joe was so upset with Ali was that he helped out Ali when he lost his boxing licence. Joe gave him money and testified in front of Congress to help get Ali's boxing licence back. Maybe Ali was just trying to hype the fights, but all the things he called Joe—like dumb, ignorant, a gorilla, and Uncle Tom—hurt him.

As we talked about whether all this stuff was staged, I got the vibe off of Joe that he didn't want to talk about Ali. So I didn't get into his fights too much. If he was nice enough to fly up from Philly to do the show (and to change the tire on the limo), I was not going to make things uncomfortable for him during the interview.

SMOKIN' JOE SINGS, CLOSED CIRCUITS, AND BRING BACK THE FAT GUY

WHEN JOE WAS CHAMPION, HE FOUGHT George Foreman in 1973. Joe was favoured in that fight, but Foreman was a lot bigger than him and things didn't go too well for Joe.

> **DON:** What was the hardest punch you ever took in your career?

> **SMOKIN' JOE:** George Foreman. Seven times, he knocked me down. George had a good punch, but he didn't have the technique to really hurt a guy.

> **DON:** George was a good fighter, but then he got it against Ali. What happened? Did he have a bad night or a bad trainer in that fight?

> **SMOKIN' JOE:** Well, you have to be taught right. He wasn't taught right. You learn your game by being taught right,

and then you can carry on. He didn't learn right, he
didn't have anybody teaching him—all he had was
a good punch.

It was a real thrill to have heavyweight champion Joe Frazier on
the *Grapevine*. If you love sports and have never been to a boxing
match, you should go.

I used to go to a lot of boxing matches at the Boston Garden.
They built the Garden back in 1928 with boxing in mind, and the
first event at the Garden was a boxing match. One time, the Bruins
practised in the afternoon and then the bull gang changed the
Garden over to boxing for a Marvelous Marvin Hagler fight.

It was early in Hagler's career, and he was one of my favourites.
The card started around 7 P.M., so I decided to stay in the dressing
room, grab a quick nap, take a sauna and watch the fights. So the
card starts and I grab two beers and head to a seat. There was a
good crowd that night, but it wasn't sold out, and because I didn't
have a ticket, I figured I'd find a seat and sit down.

As I was looking for a seat, the crowd started to recognize me.
I found a seat I liked and put the seat down. Now, I had actually
never sat in the stands at the Garden and didn't realize the seats
came back up automatically. So I put the seat down, and unbeknownst to me it pops back up and I sat down and went right to
the floor. Well, the crowd just roared.

I got up, held up my beers and yelled, "Didn't spill a drop!"

They all gave me a big cheer.

Another boxing card at the Garden was between two pretty
good up-and-coming welterweights. I forget their names, and their
careers never took off. The undercard had a lot of club fighters
who worked full-time during the day and boxed once in a while,
like the character in *Rocky*. Those club fighters always put on a
great show.

The last match before the main event, two big heavyweights
fought. I hate to call them fat, but they both were pretty out of shape.

The bell rang for the start of the first round and the two guys stood in the middle of the ring and just pounded away on each other. They went toe to toe for three rounds, and both guys were a bloody mess before the ref stopped the fight. The crowd went nuts and gave them a standing ovation.

Now the main event starts, and it was like the Manny Pacquiao–Floyd Mayweather fight. These two guys ran and danced around the ring for the first three rounds and hardly threw a punch. Between the rounds, there is dead silence. Some guy with a thick Boston accent yells, "Bring back the fat guys!" Again, the crowd gave a big cheer.

* * *

If you can't see a boxing card live, going to see it on closed-circuit is second best. I think one of the reasons boxing is on the downslide is because of home pay-per-view. You buy a fight for $50 and you kind of watch the fight. It's just not as exciting as going to an arena and seeing it live on a huge screen.

If the fight is on a Saturday night, which most are, and you order pay-per-view at home, you watch a little of the undercard, then you flip to "Coach's Corner" and then back to the fight, flip back to the hockey game and then back to the fight. It's not the same as going to, say, Maple Leaf Gardens to see the closed-circuit of Hagler and Thomas Hearns.

But one thing about going to see a closed-circuit fight: they drew a tough and sometimes violent crowd. You can be a smart-mouth at a hockey game, football game or baseball game, and 99 percent of the time nothing will happen. If you went looking for trouble at a closed-circuit event, you'd find it pretty quick.

One of the last closed-circuit fights I saw was in 1986, when Irishman Barry McGuigan defended his featherweight title against American Steve Cruz. I saw it at Varsity Arena in Toronto, which at the time was a pretty old (built in 1926) and rundown place.

The place was jammed, and let's say there weren't too many Irish Canadians in the stands cheering on Cruz. The closer it got to the main event, the drunker the crowd got. They didn't sell beer in the arena, so they must have snuck in the booze.

About two rows behind Tim and me sat this guy who looked like some kind of a professor. He had grey hair, a goatee and round wire-rimmed glasses. He had a large textbook of some kind sitting on his lap, and it was crowding the guys sitting next to him. He wasn't watching the fights on the big screen; he was looking around at the drunk fight fans and taking notes. I think he thought he was Jane Goodall, watching the chimpanzees in the jungle.

I said to Tim, "No matter what happens behind us, Tim, don't look back. Keep looking straight ahead." I knew there was going to be trouble with that professor guy.

The main event finally started, and the crowd was really rowdy. They were singing Irish songs and chanting McGuigan's name.

Now, the fight was in Las Vegas, in the parking lot of Caesar's Palace. For some reason, the fight started at 6 P.M. Vegas time. It was over 110 degrees (sorry, I don't know what this is in Celsius), and McGuigan was pouring sweat during the national anthems. Cruz was from Texas and he looked cool as a cucumber.

The first five rounds, McGuigan just pounded away at Cruz. It wasn't even a contest. But then you could see the heat was getting to McGuigan. In the middle rounds, the fight became a little closer. But then McGuigan melted under the heat in the later rounds. In the 10th round, Cruz knocked McGuigan down.

It came down to the 12th and final round. All McGuigan had to do was stay away from Cruz, and he would win the fight. But being Irish, he starts to go toe to toe with Cruz. The ref, Richard Steele, didn't even warn McGuigan about low blows, but he took a point away for a borderline low blow. Then Cruz knocked down McGuigan twice in the final two minutes.

McGuigan was ahead by two points on every judge's scorecard going into that final round, but with two knockdowns and the point taken away by the ref, McGuigan lost the fight by one point.

When they announced Cruz as the winner, Varsity Arena exploded. A guy sitting next to the professor-type guy grabbed his book and threw it at the screen. The book's spine ripped and all the pages went flying. Fights broke out everywhere. It was a grand time.

Even though the Irishmen were upset, it was a great fight and was voted the fight of the year by *Ring* magazine. That fight cost McGuigan a lot two years later. In a documentary shot in 1988, McGuigan accused his manager, Barney Eastwood, of forcing him to fight with a bad ankle and an ear injury. Eastwood sued for libel and won the case. Including court costs, he got close to $2 million; Barry McGuigan's purse for the fight was $500,000.

* * *

It was great having Smokin' Joe Frazier on the *Grapevine*. After Joe retired, he started a singing group called Joe Frazier and the Knockouts.

DON: How's the singing going?

SMOKIN' JOE: Let's just say I'm back at the gym every day.

In the first year of the *Grapevine* show, John Allan Cameron used to sing a song in the middle of the show and then at the end of the show. At the end of the Joe Frazier show, John started to sing "Proud Mary" and Joe jumped up on the stage and started singing along. You know what—he was pretty good!

I was proud to have Joe on the show. You could tell he was an honest guy. I truly believe he was personally hurt by Ali after helping Ali out when he was down.

After meeting Joe, I felt it was an honour when that sportswriter compared my Bruins with Smokin' Joe Frazier.

BOBBY ORR

We had Bobby on the show a few times, and every
time we had him on we'd get a huge crowd.

THE FIRST TIME I SAW BOBBY ORR

WE HAD BOBBY ORR ON THE show three times over the years.
We were taping the shows in the Don Cherry Sports Grill in
Mississauga when we interviewed Bobby on September 16, 1987.

Bobby was always our biggest draw. When the word got out that
he was going to be in the restaurant that day, people lined up at
noon for a 7 P.M. show. We had to lock the door, and people were
still trying to come in. Everybody wanted to see Bobby Orr.

The first time I saw Bobby was at the end of my hockey career.
I was 36 years old and I had just made a comeback with the
Rochester Americans of the AHL. It was November 23, 1971, and
we were in Boston to play the Boston Braves, the Bruins' AHL
affiliate, in the Boston Garden.

We went to the Garden for our scheduled morning skate, and the Bruins were practising before we went on the ice. All the Rochester players were standing by the glass, wanting to catch a glimpse of Bobby.

Now, you must remember at that time I had played 17 years in the minors and had been to every NHL camp at least once. I'd seen all the stars up close—Gordie Howe, Jean Béliveau, Bobby Hull (not in camp, but I saw him play)—and I had played exhibition games against some of these guys before I was sent down to the minors.

To tell you the truth, I kind of had it in the back of my mind that I'd seen them all. How much better could Orr be?

Years earlier, my brother Richard was with the Bruins in Bobby's rookie year, so he skated with him in training camp. I remember Richard called me and said, "You have to see this kid Orr. He's unbelievable. He's so far ahead of any other player I've seen."

I thought, "Yeah, yeah, sure."

When I stood by the glass that morning in the Boston Garden, I couldn't believe my eyes. I had never seen anybody skate like that before; it was like he was skating an inch off the ice. I also couldn't get over how he shot the puck with so little effort. Looking back, it must have been like when a trainer saw the horse Secretariat for the first time.

I have to admit I was like a big kid again. I went down to the Bruins pro shop and got a poster of Bobby. I asked one of my Rochester teammates, Rob Walton, whose brother Mike played for the Bruins at the time, to get Bobby to sign it.

Of course, I couldn't get him to sign it to *me*, so I got Bobby to sign it to Tim. Bobby signed it, "To Tim. Keep lifting the weights."

Tim still has the framed poster in his house today.

I also remember November 23, 1971, for another reason: we were playing the Boston Braves in the Garden and I scored the last goal of my career that night.

To say the Rochester club was struggling would be an understatement. We had a record of 8–15–3 and were last in our division.

It was the last game of a four-game road trip—four games in seven nights. We left Rochester and drove eight hours and played the Tidewater (Virginia) Wings and lost, 7–2. Bused out that night a short 90 minutes to Richmond, played the Richmond Robins the next day, and were beaten, 7–1. We bused out the next day, drove another nine hours to Providence, Rhode Island, and then played the Reds that night and made it close at 3–1. Bused out that night to Boston and played the next day.

Our record so far on the road trip was 0–3, and we had been outscored 17–4, and our coach and GM, Doug Adam, was not in a good mood.

That night, things didn't get any better. We were down 4–0 to the Braves in the third period and Adam was pissed at our top players, the guys who normally took the power play. Boston got a penalty and we went on the power play. Adam said, "Cherry, you play the point." Basically, he was telling the team, "If you can't do the job, I'm going to put a dummy like Cherry on the power play."

I had not played a shift all game and my legs were like cement. All I kept saying to myself was, "God, don't let me make a fool of myself."

The Rochester centre wins the draw back to me; I get the puck and head towards the net. I deke the Braves defenceman, fake a shot to the top left corner, and the goalie bites. I pull the puck around the goalie and slide it right along the ice in the bottom right corner. Without breaking stride, I skate right back to the bench as hard as I can and sit down.

The Garden was silent, and one of the Braves players, Garry Peters, hollered from the bench, "We better watch Number 2." (That was my number.) Both benches started to laugh. I scored and Adam was pissed—I couldn't win.

It was the greatest goal of my career, and I somehow knew it was my last.

To make a long story short, less than two months later Adam quit and made me coach. Two years later, Harry Sinden offered me the job to coach the Boston Bruins.

To tell you the truth, I didn't say yes right away. I told Harry I'd have to talk to Rose. You should have seen the look on his face.

One reason was that I was doing great in Rochester. The owners loved me, I was my own boss, and I was building a winning team. Did I really want to give all that up?

When I asked Rose, she said, "Could you live with yourself if you said no? It's the Boston Bruins. It's Bobby Orr."

I had made up my mind, so I told Harry yes the next day. I called Tim and said, "Guess what, Tim: your dad's going to coach the Boston Bruins."

Without hesitating, Tim said, "Does that mean I get to meet Bobby Orr?"

"Yes," I said, and then it sank in. "You know what? Yeah, so will I!"

THEY SAID BOBBY WAS TOO SMALL

When Bobby played, he was like a fireplug. He was six feet and 200 pounds. He was rock solid. But in his youth, Bobby was on the smaller side.

DON: Okay, you were 11 years old, you were five foot two and 110 pounds and everybody said you were too small. This is for all the smaller players out there.

BOBBY: I think hockey is one of the games a little guy can play. Stan Mikita, Dave Keon and others. But you got to have heart. If you get knocked down, you have to get back up. Hockey is one of the few games a small man can play in, so for all the young hockey players that think they're too small, it's not true. You can. Yes, hockey is one of the few sports a small player can play. You gotta love the game and learn how to play it well, but a smaller player can play in the NHL.

Bobby's right. If you look at all the sports, hockey probably has the most "smaller size" players that play in the majors. But I fear that this might slowly start to change.

Hockey Canada changed the age in which you can have checking. So now checking starts at minor bantam, which is age 13. You might think this is a good thing for smaller players, but I think it's the worst thing that could happen. Smaller players have to learn how to survive on the ice. They have to learn where the danger zones are, how to get in and out of trouble. You can't teach that stuff in practice. You have to learn it by playing.

When the kids are 10 years old, they can't skate fast and the size differential is not that great. So when bigger kids hit smaller kids, it's not that big a deal. The smaller kids learn how to protect themselves. They learn where the danger areas are on the ice.

Now the smaller kids are not learning it till they are 13 years old. At that age, the kids can skate a lot faster and the size differentials can be huge. I was at a game not too long ago and one of the 13-year-old defencemens was six foot three!

Think about it: before the rules changed, smaller kids had three or four years of learning how to survive contact on the ice as compared to the kids now. At 13 years old, the kids can't wait to hit. It's the forbidden fruit, and now they are going to hit everything in sight. The smaller kids are not going to be prepared for this and are going to get zonked, and this could drive some of the smaller players out of the game.

I remember watching the Leafs' 2015 first-round pick, Mitch Marner, play for the Don Mills Flyers in 2013. He would have been 15 years old. He was small — around five foot six, 125 pounds. Small, for sure, but he was one of the smartest players in the GTHL that year. Maybe not the best player, but the smartest player.

To give you some perspective, he was playing against some players that were over six foot two and 190 pounds. You could see that he knew how to get into position to score; he knew the danger zones. He also knew how to take out a bigger player, and most important, he knew how to take a hit. You could see he learned how to spin off a check. He learned that from a young age, not just in two years like the players today will have to. There were 18 players drafted ahead of Mitch in the OHL draft, and he went fourth overall in the NHL draft a few years later.

My fear is this: the smaller players are not going to learn how to protect themselves on the ice, and with the size difference among minor hockey players today, smaller players might not survive.

Bobby might have been small, but his talent was discovered at the early age of 13 years old, and junior hockey was tough on Bobby. It's tough on all the young players who have to leave home. It makes men out of them very quickly.

DON: Tell us about that fateful day in Gananoque.

BOBBY: Well, in those days the scouts didn't get up to Parry Sound much. At that time, the NHL teams owned the junior teams. The scouts would go around and recruit players for their respective junior teams. The Bruins owned two teams, Niagara Falls and Oshawa. The [Oshawa] Generals were starting up that year, and they needed players for the team. The Bruins went to Gananoque to scout two players.

DON: Do you remember who they went to look at?

BOBBY: Yes, they were scouting Gananoque's Tim Higgins and Rick Easton. We were in the playoffs. Baldy Cotton, Wren Blair, Mr. Adams and Milt Schmidt were there. [Baldy Cotton and Wren Blair were Boston scouts. Weston Adams owned the team. Milt Schmidt was the coach.]

DON: Wren Blair was almost sleeping at your house, trying to get you to go to Oshawa.

BOBBY: Well, at that time we would sign what you call a C-form. They didn't have a draft like they do today.

DON: It was like slavery.

BOBBY: Once you signed that C-form, you were owned by that club until they traded you or sold you or released you.

DON: Now, you went to Oshawa to play junior at 120 pounds. That must have been fun.

BOBBY: It was fun. My first junior training camp was in Niagara Falls. Niagara Falls and Oshawa trained together. I can still remember you'd give your lineup, your height, weight and position. They said, "Bobby Orr, 120 pounds, defence." Everybody laughed.

DON: Your mom, Arva, wasn't too happy [about] you leaving home at that age.

BOBBY: No. She thought I was a little young. After meeting the folks I'd be living with, she was a little more comfortable about it. It was difficult. I don't know if any of you have been homesick, but I can tell you I was homesick the first year away.

DON: I remember talking to your sister Pat. Every time you called home, you'd be crying, and then the whole family would be blubbering on the phone.

BOBBY: I was allowed to call home twice a week. I'd go up the street to a pay phone because I didn't want anyone to hear me or see me crying.

That's no joke. I was as homesick as Bobby when I was 16 years old and headed off to play for the Barrie Flyers of the Ontario Hockey Association. I was so homesick that I got physically sick and took off. I just left for home.

The Flyers called my mom when they couldn't find me. "We don't know where he is, Mrs. Cherry."

My mom said, "Oh, it's okay. He's home."

I played another year in Kingston and then headed back to Barrie. Playing hockey makes you grow up real fast.

> **DON:** In your first year in Oshawa, you drove back and forth from Parry Sound.

> **BOBBY:** That first year, I commuted. Most of your games were on the weekend, so it wasn't too bad.

> **DON:** You had to borrow a car.

> **BOBBY:** We had a lot of great friends that helped. For a time, we didn't have a car, and a lot of those friends would drive us down.

> **DON:** You couldn't practise with the team.

> **BOBBY:** No, I couldn't, so I skated in Parry Sound.

Well, it was worth the drive to Oshawa. When Bobby was 15, his second season with the Generals, he had 29 goals 72 points in 56 games. Remember, this was back when defencemen were supposed to score maybe 7 to 10 goals.

The Bruins called him a prodigy, and they were right. In a newspaper article in 1964, the headline read, BEANTOWN AWAITS HOCKEY PRODIGY'S 18TH BIRTHDAY.

March 21, 1966, is a date to be circled on the calendars of National Hockey League fans who lean towards the Boston Bruins, cellar-dwellers for the last few years. On that date, Bobby Orr is expected to sign a pro contract with the Bruins. It will also be his 18th birthday.

It goes on to talk about Bobby's junior career.

The mere fact that he was playing junior hockey at 14 was a feat in itself.

BOBBY ORR ON MINOR HOCKEY

I OFTEN MET BOBBY'S PARENTS, DOUG and Arva, and they were the salt of the earth. When you think about hardworking, honest Canadians, you can think of Doug and Arva. Bobby had good genes and got some of his hockey skill from his dad and his grandfather.

His grandfather, named Robert Orr, was a soccer player in Ballymena, Northern Ireland. Not just a run-of-the-mill player, a top-tier player at that.

Doug was no slouch, either.

DON: Tell us about Doug.

BOBBY: My dad tells me he was a pretty good hockey player. When he was 16, he was invited to two camps, the Leafs and Bruins camp, but he joined the navy instead. He came home from the navy, was married, and that was it.

DON: He served on a corvette and patrolled the North Atlantic for subs. Now, when did your dad start you skating?

BOBBY: I think I started skating when I was three or four on a rink beside our house.

DON: Did he ever push you?

BOBBY: No, I was never pushed. He made sure I had equipment and drove me to the games and so on. But I was never pushed to play. I was never told, "You're going to be a hockey player." I always had fun and enjoyed it. Never any pressure.

Bobby's father, Doug, never pressured him, Bobby loved to play. You can say that about all the players in the NHL. They all must have a love of the game and a desire to get to the pros.

When I'm out scouting the minor midgets with Tim, you can tell the players who don't love the game and are playing for their parents. You can see that they don't have the same desire as the rest of the kids. But those kids are few and far between. Even to make it to minor midget AAA in the Greater Toronto Hockey League, you have to have a love of the game and the desire to play.

One thing that really bugs me about the media: when they report on minor hockey, they always seem to try and paint a picture of kids not wanting to go to the game or practice and the parents dragging them kicking and screaming to the rinks.

Nothing could be further from the truth. You see the kids coming to the rink in their shirts and ties with their team jackets on. There is a sense of pride with the kids. A sense that they are proud to play hockey and be part of a team.

I know I talked about this before, but a big part of that is wearing shirts and ties. I know some people laugh when I say that. But I know it to be true. I talk to the parents and they tell me that it's a big deal for the kids to go shopping for a shirt and tie to get ready for the season. It teaches the kids to respect themselves and the game. It teaches them to get ready for the game. Not just wear some jeans and an old hoodie and head out to the rink.

You're going to play hockey, not going over to friends to play video games. It tells the kids to get ready; you're doing something important.

How many times does a 10-year-old kid wear a shirt and tie if he doesn't play hockey? Not many. I see kids now dressed in full suits at the rink.

I was at a tournament and the North York Ranger players all had matching suits and ties. They looked dynamite. I see some kids now with bow ties and suits with vests. You can see they have pride in themselves.

I talked to one father. His son was a big, good-looking kid with his suit and tie on. He looked like a model.

I said, "Your son looks like a pro hockey player with his suit on."

His father shook his head and said, "I don't like it when he wears his suit to the game."

To tell you the truth, I got mad and was about to give him hell—"Why don't you want your son looking like a million dollars coming to the game?"

The father, straight-faced, said, "When he wears his suit to the game, he always asks me to carry his bag because he doesn't want to wrinkle his pants."

I always like to show the NHLers walking into the rink, all dressed up, on "Coach's Corner." It shows the kids that the pros wear a shirt and tie, so they should be like the pros.

I did get in trouble one time when I showed the first-place Pittsburgh Penguins walking into the rink in Ottawa. Sidney Crosby looked like he just walked of the pages of GQ. Then I showed the Senators players walking in, and they looked awful. No shirts and ties, and they had stupid-looking hats on.

I said, "Now look at Pittsburgh and Crosby. First-place team and best player in the NHL. You dress like a winner and you play like a winner. Now look at Ottawa—last-place club and look how they dress. Dress like a loser and you'll play like a loser. They look like a bunch of thugs."

The CBC got a letter from the Senators, and they wanted an apology for calling the players thugs.

I told the CBC, "I didn't say they were thugs. I said they *looked like* thugs."

That was the end of that.

I know some do-gooders want this stopped. They say it's too expensive to wear shirts and ties. Look, if you can put your kid through hockey and buy him a team jacket, you can afford to go to Walmart and buy a shirt and tie. I have heard that the word has come down in some leagues that if you wear a shirt and tie, you get suspended. It's sad. It's part of our heritage, and now some people want to get rid of it because of some misguided politically correct idea.

I was at a tournament a few years ago and a team of 10-year-old players came up for pictures. None of them had shirts or ties. I looked at them funny and didn't say anything. They left and another team came up, all looking sharp.

I said, "Now, here comes some hockey players. You guys look great. I don't know about that last team. They aren't dressed as sharp as you guys."

I'll never forget, one of the players, with such a look of contempt on his face, said, "Yeah, Grapes, they're from Detroit."

* * *

There's one thing I always wonder. With Bobby's skating and the way he can score, how come he played defence? It was unheard of back in the day for a defenceman to score a lot.

DON: Royce Tennant and Bucko McDonald. They are the guys that put you on the road.

BOBBY: They coached in the minor hockey leagues in Parry Sound. They were great coaches. Their philosophy was to teach the kids fundamentals and make sure the kids have fun. If kids have fun, they are going to continue to play the game, and if they are playing, we can teach them so much. Royce was the guy that put me on defence.

DON: You used to play forward.

BOBBY: I don't know why Royce wanted me to play defence. That's where he thought I should play.

DON: Worked out all right. When you were skating on the rinks, how long did you go? Doug would say, "You skated all by yourself under the moon."

BOBBY: We had a very large minor hockey organization in Parry Sound and we had to wait our turn. We did most of our skating in the outdoors. The school rink, parking lots, and on the weekend we'd play from morning till night. That's where we learned all our skills. Without adults, just dropping the puck and go. These systems are too much.

DON: You used to hollow out a puck and filled it full of lead.

BOBBY: That's how I practised. Shoot at a piece of plywood and set up another piece of plywood with targets on it.

DON: For how long?

BOBBY: Oh, for hours. I'd dig out the puck and put lead in it to make it heavier and a little harder to shoot.

DON: You know what bothers me, Bobby, and God love 'em, I'm not knocking the coaches, they get up at five in the morning, but what bothers me is when I go to the practices and I hear the coaches yelling, "Pass it. Pass it." I mean, if you would have done that, you wouldn't have made it.

BOBBY: Like I said, we learned our skills with 10 or 15 players on each team, just drop the puck and go. That's how we learned to skate and that's how we learned to handle the puck. I don't see that much anymore. I think in many cases, the kids would be much better off if they went out on their own, not waiting for the adults to organize it. Just go out and play. I don't see much sandlot baseball anymore; you don't see the kids often playing hockey on the street. That's where we learned our skill.

DON: Did you have any special drills?

BOBBY: I'm not sure I could play today. All I keep hearing about is systems. On the outdoor rinks, we learned the fundamentals of the skating, shooting, puck handling, passing—the basic fundamentals of the game. A youngster . . . how much can he understand about systems? There comes a time when he's old enough and can understand the systems and so on. For the young ones, at least, they should just be learning the basic fundamentals.

The funny thing is, when I'm out scouting, the first things scouts ask about a young hockey player is "Can he skate?" The second thing they ask is "Can he handle the puck?" It seems nowadays that's being driven out of the game. Sad.

FIRST GUY TO MAKE THE BIG DOUGH

BOBBY NOT ONLY CHANGED THE WAY the game was played, he changed the way players were paid. Bobby ushered in the era of the offensive defenceman. Before him, hardly any defencemen rushed with the puck, and not many scored a lot of points.

As we all know, Bobby was the first and last defenceman to lead the NHL in points. In the 1969–70 season, Bobby led all players in points with 120—33 goals and 87 assists. Not only that, he still had over 125 minutes in penalties, and that included seven fighting majors, so he was no sweetheart.

Oh yeah, and that year he won the Art Ross, Hart, Conn Smythe and Norris Trophies and the Stanley Cup.

We had Gump Worsley on the show with Bobby one year, and I asked if he ever scored on Gump. Bobby said his first NHL goal was against Gump.

Gump laughed, "So what else is new? Half the NHL scored their first goal on me."

> **DON:** First guy to make the big dough in the National Hockey League. How much did you get your rookie year?

Bobby started to laugh.

> **BOBBY:** Compared to what they get now, not that much. I think my salary back then was about $15,000, and if I played 40 games I got a $5,000 bonus. In my second year, I got $20,000, and if I played 40 games I got $5,000. At that time, it was a lot.

> **DON:** Today, for Scott Stevens, that's walking-around money. But after that, the salaries took right off.

> **BOBBY:** It took a few more years before the salaries started to escalate. Today, the players, good luck to them. It does not bother me to see players making big money. What bothers me is the player that is making the big money, and you go see him play and he disappoints you. That happens quite a bit. I don't mind them making that money, but you need to perform.

Gretzky, Yzerman, those guys never disappoint you. They come to play every night.

DON: How did the players receive you in your rookie year?

BOBBY: I can remember my first camp like it was yesterday. We were training in London, Ontario. I walked into my room. There was a gentleman laying on the bed, just in his shorts, and a little tummy on him—he looked like Buddha. He was smoking a big cigar. I looked at him and I recognized him and said, "Hello, Mr. Bucyk." He laughed and said, "Call me Chief."

Of course, he was talking about Johnny Bucyk. He was the captain of the Bruins and played 23 seasons in the NHL. So Bobby was making around $20,000 in 1966. I was playing in Rochester and was making around $5,000.

OFF TO A BIT OF A ROCKY START, AND TRADING PHIL

I WOULD LIKE TO SAY BOBBY and I hit it off right from the start. I guess I tried too hard, and I must admit I was in awe of him, which is not good for a coach.

So in my first training camp as coach of the Bruins, I saw Bobby eating breakfast all by himself. I hadn't really talked to him, and I thought I'd better say hello and strike up a conversation. You have to remember, I was a minor-league player and had coached two years in the AHL. Bobby was now considered the greatest player in the game, if not the whole history of the NHL.

I've always liked to fish, and I'd heard Bobby liked to fish too. I asked him about the fishing around Parry Sound. What a phony I was. He saw right through it and was cool to me.

I quickly realized what I did wrong, and I never made that mistake again.

To say Bobby is intense is an understatement. All great hockey players have that intensity, even off the ice, and Bobby had it in spades. Rocket Richard was like that; you could feel the vibe off him that you didn't fool around with him.

Bobby didn't suffer fools and wouldn't put up with nonsense in the dressing room. He doesn't know I know this story, but Ron MacLean told me something that happened in my first practice as coach of the Bruins that I had no idea about at the time.

Ron was talking to someone who was in the dressing room that day. He told Ron that everybody was on the ice, but Phil Esposito was late. Bobby quietly went off the ice and went back into the dressing room. "It's our new coach's first practice and you're late. Get your ass on the ice now!" Bobby growled at Phil.

As intense as Bobby was off the ice and during practice, it was amplified times 10 during a game. I found the best way to coach him was just to let him do his thing, and I learned that the hard way.

We were playing an exhibition game in Moncton, New Brunswick. During the first period, Bobby was on the ice for a goal. He came to the bench just seething. It was an exhibition game in front of 5,000 people, but that made no difference to Bobby. He had fire coming out of eyes, he was so mad.

The next shift, he got the puck and went through the whole team and put a laser in the top corner, and then he skated right to the bench, still seething.

Now, it was one of my first games as coach and I was not too sure how to handle him. The crowd was going wild and the players were banging the boards with their sticks.

I figured I should acknowledge the goal. I said, very innocently, "Nice goal, Bobby."

He said—again, he was still in a rage from the play before— "Oh gee, thanks, Coach, thanks."

I was in shock, but it taught me a lesson: just let him go and do his thing. He potted 46 goals, 135 points, over 100 minutes in penalties, had a plus/minus of plus 128, led the NHL in points, won the Art Ross and Norris.

* * *

I had a good regular season my first year with Boston. We were fourth overall in the league, with a record of 40–26–14 for 94 points. The first round of the playoffs that year was best two games out three, which is a killer. We faced Chicago the first round, and they didn't have a bad club. They had won 34 games and had a wild card in their goalie, Tony Esposito.

I was confident going into the first game of the series. And the first game, with Tony in net, we hammered Chicago, 8–2. It was no contest. The next day in the Boston papers, the headlines were TONY ESPOSITO FINISHED — HANG IT UP, TONY. My heart sank. I knew Tony had a lot of pride and a lot of game left in him.

I wanted to finish off Chicago the next game. I didn't want to face Tony in a sudden-death game. We lost in Chicago, 4–3 in overtime. Ivan Boldirev scored about seven minutes into sudden-death and we headed back to the Garden. Just what I feared would happen, happened. In the first period, after we poured 19 shots on Tony, we're losing 2–0. At the end of the game, we outshot Chicago by 37 shots. The finals shots on goal were 56–19, and we lost, 6–4. Tony just killed us.

I was sitting in my office after the game, still in shock. Bobby, still in his equipment and sweat pouring off him, quietly came in and sat down. After a moment of silence, he said, "Grapes, I didn't play good for you."

Can you imagine? Leading the league in goals and points, and in the three games in the playoffs he had six points.

That's the kind of player he was. He took every loss personally.

A quick side note to this story. A lot of people ask me why Gilles Gilbert, my starting goalie in my rookie year of coaching, and I never really got along.

My first game as head coach of Boston was in Buffalo. Gilles starts and we get hammered, 9–5. I can't believe it. I hear Gilles in the dressing room say to the trainer, "Well, that's it for me. My average is never going to be good this year."

My first game, we give up nine goals, and my starting goalie says that's it for him for the season.

The season ended just as badly. Gilles was in net for the 6–4 loss to the Hawks. Tony stopped 52 shots and Gilles let in six goals on 19 shots. He was later quoted in the paper, saying, "All those goals were good tonight . . . Tony played well and we hit a few posts. But the 56 shots are a little deceptive. Many of them were long ones . . . not good percentage shots."

Needless to say, the next year we got Gerry Cheevers back from the WHA and Gilles was the backup. But with all that, Gilly still set a record in the 1975–76 season that stands today for longest winning streak by a goalie in one season, with 17 straight wins without a loss.

The next season, 1975–76, was when Bobby really got mad at me. Bobby was out for the start of the season and we were struggling. He was scheduled to come back against Vancouver, 12 games into the season. For those 12 games, we had a 5–5–2 record.

That was not going to do for the Bruins fans. Getting knocked out in the first round of the playoffs the year before and struggling as we were, I thought Harry Sinden could do one of two things. He could fire me or shake up the team with a big trade.

He told the press and me right after the playoffs that I was his coach. Sometimes that's the kiss of death, but I believed him. Harry wanted to change the way the team played. The Bruins for years were an offensive juggernaut, and Harry wanted the team to play more defensive.

I think Harry liked the way I coached because I was a guy who had a defensive system. I had only three rules when I coached the Bruins.

First, do what you want in their end. I don't care what you do. I always thought to myself, "How am I going to tell Phil Esposito or Johnny Bucyk how to score goals?"

Second, in our end, you do exactly as I say. I wanted the wingers to cover the points and the defence to hammer the puck around the boards as soon as they touched it—except for Bobby, of course. The wingers were to make sure the puck got out of our end. I always wanted a winger back. Nowadays, the "experts" call it the left-wing lock. I had my wingers back in a defensive role so there would be no odd-man rushes. So the left-wing lock, as Ron MacLean would call it, was being done back in the '70s. It is not something coaches invented the last few years.

Third, and most important, remember: when Orr has the puck, don't go offside.

Harry knew that with the makeup of the team, we'd never get the players to change their ways. So the only option was to shake up the team. Harry talked to me about it during the summer, and with us struggling at the start of the season, we needed to make a move. We had just lost to Buffalo, 4–0, and then headed out to Vancouver.

When I arrived, Harry called me and said he was about to make the trade for New York's Brad Park, Jean Ratelle and Joe Zanussi for Phil Esposito and Carol Vadnais.

When Harry asked my opinion, I told him to make the trade. I knew that having Brad Park, the second-best defenceman in the league behind only Bobby, we'd win the Stanley Cup. I had no doubt.

Harry called to tell me the trade was done, but the New York papers somehow got wind of it and were breaking the story first thing in the morning. Harry told me I had to tell Phil and Carol before they read it in the papers.

I called Bobby and told him we had to meet Phil in his room. We knocked on the door, Phil saw Bobby and me standing there, and he knew something was up. He thought I'd been fired. Bobby walked to the window and looked out over the Vancouver harbour.

"Phil, you've been traded," I told him straight out.

He was in shock. No one saw this coming. Phil had just signed a three-year deal with Boston for less money than he could have gotten in the WHA, so he had no idea that Harry would even consider trading him. He sat down and had tears in his eyes. Boston had a huge Italian community, and Phil was their hero. It was going to be hard for him to leave Boston.

He looked up at me and said, "Grapes, if you tell me I've been traded to New York, I'm going to jump out that window."

For the life of me, I don't know why I said this: "Bobby, get away from that window."

Here a guy's life has been rocked, and I have to be a smart-ass.

I then had to go tell Carol Vadnais. Carol was one of the classiest guys in hockey, and I consider him one of my good friends. It was just as tough telling Carol he was traded. Like Phil, he was in shock, but he took it very calmly.

Then he said, "Grapes, they can't trade me."

I said, "Vad, I know it's tough, but—"

He said, "No, not that. They can't trade me. I have a no-trade clause in my contract."

I called Harry right away from Carol's room, and he picked up the phone on the first ring. "How did Phil take it?" he asked.

"He's not happy, but we have a problem with Vad. He says he has a no-trade clause in his contract."

Harry had Carol's contract right in front of him, and I could hear him flipping pages, and then the pages stopped turning. "I'll call you back," he said and slammed the phone down.

I realized that Carol did have a no-trade clause in his contract, and he could refuse a trade. I said to him, "Look, Vad, you could go to New York. They really want you, and you could ask for extra money to waive the no-trade clause."

I guess Vad must have thought, "Well, if they are going to trade me now, they are going to try to trade me later." He agreed to the trade, made some extra dough and went on to score 20 goals for the Rangers that season, his best year ever. Later, he became the Rangers' assistant coach.

I knew with Park and Orr on the points, we'd be Stanley Cup champs. I had no doubt about it. We were staying at the Bayshore Hotel in Vancouver and they had a beautiful bar in the lobby.

I went there after I had talked to Phil and Carol and had a beer. The place was empty. Perfect.

I was wearing my Calder Cup championship ring. I was looking at it when the bartender handed me another beer. "See this ring here?" I said. "This is a championship ring from the American Hockey League. At the end of the season, I'll be wearing a Stanley Cup ring instead."

He looked at me a little strange. Little did I know that the hockey fates had something else in store for me.

When the trade was announced, the Boston papers were not happy. They said Rangers GM Emile Francis robbed Harry. The Bruins fans were going nuts on the radio, calling for Harry's and my head.

One thing that made the trade hard for the Boston fans was that they hated Brad Park. One of our oldest veterans and a good friend of Phil trashed his hotel room.

Next day, when I went to the dressing room for the morning skate, the feeling in the room was like someone had just died. I started to get pissed off. I knew Phil and Vad were friends of many of the Bruins players, but if we didn't start winning, I was going to lose my job. We weren't winning, so too bad we had to trade their friends.

I went on the ice after all the players had gone on. They were skating around, and then Bobby skated up to me, seething. "Did you have anything to do with this trade?"

I shot back, "Damn [I've cleaned up the language for our younger readers] right, Bobby."

"Why didn't you wait till I came back?" he said and skated away.

I blew the whistle for the players to speed up. Nothing. I blew it again. Nothing. Here was the moment of truth. If I didn't straighten this out fast, I would lose the team. I was in a rage when I called everybody over to the far corner, away from the benches, where the press was waiting. I didn't want the press to hear that we were having a little rebellion.

I smashed my stick and said, "Listen, you guys [again I'll clean up the language here]: Phil and Vad are gone. There's nothing you can do about it. If we can trade Phil and Vad, we can trade anybody on this team. Now, when I blow the whistle to speed up, you'd better speed up or you'll be gone, too."

They sped up after the next whistle.

Brad and Jean made it out for the game in Vancouver and we lost, 4–2. Harry called me right away after the game. Because we lost to Vancouver, not even a .500 club, the fans were in more of a frenzy. "Harry, calm down," I said. "I saw something. We're going to be great."

Harry barked back, "We'd better, or both of us are going to be fired."

The next night, we were playing the California Seals. We were losing halfway through the first and were all a little panicky. If we lost this game, there was a good chance I might get fired—maybe even Harry too.

Bobby got the puck behind our net and stopped. He looked at the bench and the players on the ice as if to say, "OK everybody, calm down."

It seemed to turn things around. We won, 6–3, and headed back to Boston. We played OK the first two games, but in between the two games we didn't have time to really have Ratelle and Park practise with their new team. We had a few days off and I could see Orr and Park getting more comfortable with each other on the ice and on the power play. The fans were still in upset and were just looking for us to stumble.

We played Minnesota at the Garden and we won, 6–0, thank goodness. Orr and Park were magic on the power play. Minnesota had a great goalie named Cesare Maniago, and we poured 46 shots against him. I remember he called a time out and took his mask off and leaned against the net.

The Boston fans gave him a standing ovation for his effort. He later said that with Park and Orr, it was like facing two cannons on the point.

The team took off. Bobby had scored eight points in his first three games back. Park and Ratelle were fitting in perfectly and we didn't look back. In fact, we only lost one of our next 19 games.

After the loss in Vancouver, our winning percentage was .462. Nineteen games later, our winning percentage was .656. Needless to say, the fans soon were happy with the trade.

Then the hockey gods turned. We played LA at the Garden, won 4–2, and headed to New York to play the Rangers on a Wednesday. Bobby scored his last goal as a Bruin in that game.

The Rangers' goalie, John Davidson, made a terrific save on Bobby, robbing him of a goal. Bobby was mad, and a few shifts later he roared up the ice and let a rocket go. It was as if he was saying, "This puck is getting past you or through you."

Davidson flashed out his glove and caught the puck. It was such a hard shot, it almost ripped the glove off of his hand, and he fell back into the net with the puck. With a goal and an assist, it was Bobby's best game since coming back. In his 10 games, he scored 18 points. We went on to win, 6–4.

Inside Madison Square Garden, there is a ramp you have to walk down to get on the bus. After the game, Bobby was walking down the ramp and he felt a twinge in his knee. I asked Bobby if he was okay.

"Yeah, I just tweaked my knee."

We both didn't think anything of it.

On Friday, November 28, we were boarding a plane to Chicago. I was always the last guy to board, and as I was heading down the ramp, some of the players were carrying Bobby off the plane.

"Grapes, my knee locked on me," he said.

He seemed fine in practice the day before, and I hoped it wasn't serious. I was wishing that some physio or something like that would be good enough to fix it, but it was not to be.

The next day, Bobby had an operation on his left knee.

That was it. Bobby was out for the season, and he went to Chicago the next year. I couldn't believe how fast Bobby had gone under the knife.

I started getting calls in my hotel room in Chicago from the Boston press. "If there's anybody in sports that can come back from this, it's Bobby Orr," I told them.

The doctors said he'd be out for six weeks, but he had to call it a season. We went on to have a .706 winning percentage, first place in the Adams Division, and went to the semifinals.

I will tell you again: if Bobby didn't get hurt, we would have won the Stanley Cup.

As we all know, Bobby had to retire at the age of 30, just at the age when defencemen are coming into their own.

DON: So, when did you first hurt your knee?

BOBBY: I believe it was in my rookie season. I believe it was Marcel Pronovost, and it was a clean check. I was going down the boards and I was trying to slip by Marcel; I went by him kind of sideways. I pinned my leg against the boards.

When you watch old videos of Bobby, he was so fast that guys couldn't time the hit right and were always a bit late on the hit. Because of that, they caught Bobby on the leg or they would stick their legs out to try and get a piece of him. Bobby would also get the puck and go into traffic.

Most players would try and go around guys; Bobby would go right through them. The only other player I've seen that happen to was Pavel Bure. He was so fast, guys couldn't catch him, so they just got pieces of him and just caught his leg.

We all know Pavel had to retire because of knee injuries.

THE MYSTIQUE OF BOBBY ORR

I WAS ONCE ASKED IN AN interview why is there such a mystique around Bobby. I think there are two reasons.

First, Bobby went out on top. I don't mean winning a championship and then retiring. I mean he was at his best. As I stated, he retired when most defencemen are hitting their prime. His last full season, he led the league in assists and points and scored 46 goals. His best year ever.

Most superstars always play a little too long. They love the game, like Bobby did, and have a tough time letting it go. But with Bobby retiring at age 30, we'll never know how good he could have been, and that's hard to believe.

How many more Stanley Cups would he have won? I'd say at least three. I believe we would have beat Montreal at least two out of the three series we played against them in the '70s.

Like the great Montreal defenceman Serge Savard said, "There are players, there are stars, there are superstars, and then there is Bobby Orr."

The second reason is that the fans didn't see a lot of Bobby as compared to today's superstars, and I think that adds a lot to the mystique. Remember, when he played, there were no 24-hour sports stations, and you could only get the Bruins games if you lived around Boston. The nightly news didn't show all the highlights.

Today, every game is on TV. Every goal and save is shown 10 times on the sports stations and talked about on 24-hour sports radio. Sometimes I think it's too much. Because Bobby wasn't overexposed, when the fans saw him, they went nuts.

There were a lot of instances of fans going wild for Bobby, but I'll tell you one of my favourite stories.

We were playing an exhibition game in Providence, Rhode Island. The owner of the Providence Reds, the AHL team there, advertised with the slogan "Come see Bobby Orr." Again, remember that most of the fans coming to the game didn't have a lot of chances to see Bobby live or on television. So seeing him play live was a huge deal. The place sold out in minutes.

I hated playing Bobby in exhibition games because he wouldn't take it easy; he played all out. I also didn't want some idiot taking a run at him to try and make a name for himself.

The place was jammed even before we took the ice. Fans wanted to see the warm-up to get a glimpse of Bobby. The game started, and I'm not really sure what happened, but Bobby got into a fight and wouldn't stop. I can't remember the ref, but he gave Bobby a game misconduct five minutes into the game.

Bobby skated over to the bench and said, "I'm gone," and headed to the dressing room.

I was happy as a pig in mud. I didn't want him to play anyway. Bobby leaves, and you can start to hear a buzz going around the rink. I look up to see a guy run down the stairs from the press box and jump into the timekeeper's box. I can't hear what he's saying, but he's going nuts, screaming at the ref.

They started to announce the penalties, and then they stopped. The crowd now started to get the idea that Bobby was gone, and there was an edge in the air. Some fans started booing and throwing things on the ice. The guy running down the stairs and jumping into the timekeeper's box was the owner of the Reds. He was screaming at the ref, "Are you crazy? We have 5,000 people here to see Bobby Orr and you throw him out in the first five minutes? Bring him back or we're going to have a riot on our hands."

He was right. Fans were throwing things and screaming and yelling. The ref skated over and said to me, "I'm not giving him a game misconduct. Tell Bobby to come back."

I looked at him and said, "No."

You could see the panic in his eyes. "Grapes, do me a favour and tell him to come back. There's going to be a riot!"

I thought about it and went back into the dressing room. He was already getting into the shower. "Bobby, get dressed," I said. "You have to come back."

You should have seen the look on his face. "No. He gave me a misconduct. I'm not going back." I had to explain that the fans were starting to riot and he'd better come back or the place was going to explode. So he got dressed—not happy, I might add— and played the rest of the game and gave it his best as usual.

* * *

I always look back at my time coaching Bobby with a mixture of happiness and a bit of sadness. I was honoured that I was coaching when Bobby, the greatest hockey player who ever lived, had his greatest year. We had a lot of fun. But I then feel a bit sad because I think what the team could have done, how many Stanley Cups we would have won, if Bobby had played three or four more years.

But then I get to thinking: nobody saw Bobby on the way down like with most athletes. Like I said, think about the last full season he played: he scored 46 goals, 135 points, he still got over 100 penalty minutes, a plus/minus of plus 124, won the Art Ross, Norris and Lester B. Pearson Trophies.

Bobby's last triumph was in 1976, when he went to the Canada Cup (which they now call the World Cup) in Montreal. That Team Canada was the greatest team ever assembled.

Of course we won the championship, beating the Czechs in the finals. Bobby was playing on one knee and he still was tied for the tournament lead with nine points in seven games. He was the tournament MVP. His knee was bothering him the whole series.

Bobby Clarke said, "Orr is better on one knee than the rest of us with two good knees. He deserved the MVP. There should be a higher league that he can go and play in."

He then went to Chicago and played only 24 games in three years. Everybody, including myself, remembers Bobby as a shooting star, shining brightly at the top of his game.

That's how it should be.

TOMMY KNIGHT

Tommy Knight and Tim.
Tommy had a scary run-in with a wrestler.

TOMMY VS. THE WRESTLER

WE USED THE CREWS AT CHCH-TV in Hamilton for the tapings. They were all great guys and gals and we had a lot of fun doing the shows. One person in particular, floor director Tommy Knight, was a real big help to me. Tommy was the guy who would tell me how much time we had left in the interview and would let me know what was going on. If I got mad, Tommy would calm me down, and if I had a question, Tommy would know the answer.

Besides the *Grapevine* shows, the crew at CHCH did a lot of different events. They shot a lot of the Buffalo Sabres games as well as a lot of the Leafs games, which they aired on Wednesday nights. One of the other shows they taped at Maple Leaf Gardens was wrestling.

Now, wrestling was in its heyday at that time, and wrestlers were as popular as any other athletes. One day, Tim and Tommy were talking, and Tim was wondering if we should try to get a wrestler on the *Grapevine*. There were some Canadian wrestlers who were making it big, and it might be fun to get them on the show. The CHCH crew was shooting *Maple Leaf Wrestling* that weekend, and Tommy said he'd ask around and see if any of the wrestlers wanted to come on the show.

So before the wrestling show at Maple Leaf Gardens started, Tommy was in the private dressing room of a very popular wrestler who was Canadian. We are not mentioning his name so as to protect the guilty. Tommy was setting up a monitor in the room and he asked if the wrestler had ever heard of the *Grapevine* shows. The wrestler said yes, he'd heard of the show and was a fan of Don Cherry. So naturally, Tommy asked if he'd like to come on as a guest. Well, the wrestler got upset and started to scream and yell. He grabbed Tommy, who's about five foot five, and pinned him against the wall and then started to toss him around the room.

The wrestler was saying things like "Nobody can make me do things I don't want" and "If I don't want to go on, no one can make me," all the time pushing Tommy around. The wrestler then opened the door and threw Tommy out into the hall.

As you can imagine, Tommy was pretty shook up. One of the wrestling executives saw Tommy standing in the hall and asked what happened. Tommy explained, and the executive apologized. At the end of the day, Tommy and the crew were packing up to leave and the executive told Tommy that the wrestler wanted to see him in his dressing room. Tommy goes back to the scene of the crime, and the wrestler explained to Tommy that he was under a lot of pressure and that he shouldn't have grabbed him.

Tommy said, "I understand. I guess I shouldn't have asked that of you. But apology accepted." The wrestler turned to Tommy and said, "Who are you that I have to apologize? I'm not apologizing to you!" He goes on another rant and grabs Tommy and throws him around the room again and then out the door.

Safe to say, we never had a wrestler come on the *Grapevine* show.

MAURICE RICHARD

Having the Rocket on the show was like having royalty on the show.
His eyes still had the "don't fool with me" fire in them.

THE FIRST TIME I MET MAURICE RICHARD,
AND HOW HE BECAME THE ROCKET

I FIRST MET—I REALLY DIDN'T MEET him, so I guess you could
say the first time I *saw*—the Rocket in person was in the 1955
Stanley Cup playoffs. It was Game 5 of the semifinals between
the Bruins and Canadiens, and I was about to play what would be,
unbeknownst to me, my one and only game in the NHL.

Before the game, I was getting ready in the Bruins dressing room
when defenceman Hal Laycoe went on a rant. He was throwing
sticks and yelling, "There is no way I'm standing, honouring that
guy. He carved me up with his stick and I'm going to stand at the
blue line honouring him?"

The Rocket had hit Laycoe over the head during the season in
a vicious fight. Those two had something going. Laycoe was in the
middle of the action when the Rocket knocked out a linesman,

and the NHL president, Mr. Clarence Campbell, suspended him for the rest of the season and the playoffs, but more about that later.

After Laycoe went nuts in the dressing room, our coach, Milt Schmidt, said, "OK, Cherry, you start instead of Laycoe." So I got to stand at the blue line, honouring the Rocket. I didn't mind. He never corked *me* with his stick.

It was crazy at the Forum that night. When Mr. Campbell suspended the Rocket, with three games left in the regular season, he was leading the NHL in scoring. Bernie "Boom Boom" Geoffrion was a few points behind him. While the Rocket was sitting out those last three games of the season, Boom Boom went on to beat the Rocket by one point. He had 38 goals and 37 assists, while the Rocket had 38 goals and 36 assists. Jean Béliveau came in third, with 73 points, just one point behind the Rocket.

Let me tell you what kind of player the Rocket was. He had over 120 minutes in penalties, while Boom Boom had 57 PIMs and Béliveau had 58. Before this game, the Canadiens wanted to honour Geoffrion for winning the Art Ross Trophy for top scorer. There were always rumours, and I believe them, that Béliveau didn't want to score any points in those last three games because he wanted the Rocket to win the scoring title. He knew how much it meant to the Montreal fans. When they introduced Boom Boom, the fans booed him because he beat out their beloved Rocket.

They then introduced the Rocket, acknowledging him for coming in second in the scoring, and the fans went wild. Never mind that Bernie was a Montreal Canadien, he beat out the most-loved guy in Quebec. This was the only time the Rocket had a chance to win a scoring title, and the fans let Bernie know about their displeasure.

When the Rocket came out onto the ice, it was something to see and hear the fans, how much they loved him. I still remember they gave him an electric iron—the kind you iron your clothes with—as a gift for coming in second in the scoring race.

The Rocket took this all in stride. He smiled and waved to the fans. He was like a god in Quebec.

I thought, "This NHL is something. Laycoe going nuts in the dressing room before the game and fans booing a player on their own team for winning the scoring championship."

This would be my one and only game in the NHL. My mother and my aunt Tilley were in the stands, watching. I played a regular shift and even knocked down Béliveau. We lost the game and the Bruins were out of the playoffs.

After the game, I met my mom and aunt and they gave me a shopping bag full of cookies. The Bruins went to a bar after the game, and we all had a few beers while eating my mother's cookies.

* * *

Almost 30 years later, the Rocket was a guest on our second year of the *Grapevine*. I was always nervous doing the shows, but I was extra nervous with the Rocket as a guest. When he walked into the studio to do the show, it honestly felt like royalty. Not that he put on airs or anything like that; it was just his presence. The Rocket had a quiet dignity about him, the way he walked. It was just the way he carried himself. There was something there that I can't put into words.

The only person I had the same feeling with was Jean Béliveau. The only difference between Jean and the Rocket was that with the Rocket, there seemed to be a violence simmering behind his eyes. There was an intensity, even when he was relaxed. Bobby Orr is the same way; there is a simmering intensity that could explode at any moment.

I remember Rocket had a friend with him who was his buffer. Not a bodyguard or handler; he just took care of the mundane stuff. In the first year of the *Grapevine* shows, Ralph Mellanby and Gerry Patterson were the executive producers, and they told the Rocket's friend what was going to happen.

The friend took the Rocket aside and went over the situation, and we could see the Rocket relax. Evidently, he had been burned a couple of times in interviews. Once that happens to a guy like the Rocket, he's always going to have his guard up. The interview turned out to just be two hockey guys together, one a superstar and one a minor leaguer who, you could tell, thought the world of him. I felt the Rocket knew there was no way I was going to try and trick him, and he even started to smile and laugh during the show. After the show, his friend told Ralph that the Rocket had enjoyed the show more than any other interview he had done, French or English. That made me feel good, I'll tell ya.

* * *

We had broadcaster Dick Beddoes sitting in the audience, and he was the second interview that night. Dick was a great guy and one of the best sports broadcasters ever. Before we started Rocket's interview, Dick and I chatted about the great Number 9. He was always trying to take over the show when you were on the air with him.

> **DICK:** You got a star tonight on your show. His eyes—when we talk about the Rocket's red glare, that's what we're talking about. He was a fiery competitor and nobody came across centre ice like the Rocket. He could fly.

> **DON:** I got a few stats here. Now, listen to this. This was back when they checked. Remember, a lot of the games were 2–1, 3–2.

> **DICK:** A lot of 1–0 games too.

> **DON:** Now, listen to these stats. OK, everybody knows he was the first guy to score 50 goals and he did it in 50 games. Everyone knows Gretzky broke that one. This is just some of his records. Twenty-six hat tricks. Now, this is the one I like, shows he was a clutch guy: 82 game-winning goals. Now, in

the playoffs: seven hat tricks in the playoffs, and how about six playoff overtime goals. In 133 playoff games, 82 goals and 18 game-winning goals. In one game against Toronto in the playoffs, the score was 5–1 and he scored every goal. Do you remember that, Dick?

DICK: Indeed. And Don, after that game was over, they picked the three stars, and third star Richard, second star Richard and the first star Richard. Never happened before.

Then the interview with Rocket started, and I can still see those black eyes at the start of the interview focused on mine. They were almost saying, "Don't fool with me." As Dick said, they were like fire. I can only imagine what those eyes were like when he was roaring down the ice for a goal. When I started, I was kind of nervous.

DON: Hello, Rocket. Ya know, Frank Selke told me the Rocket is not God in Montreal, but he's the Pope.

I think Rocket got a little embarrassed by that.

DON: The Rocket is the greatest nickname in sports. How did you get the nickname "the Rocket"?

ROCKET: Oh, that's a long story. The first year in Montreal, I got hurt and didn't play much that year. The second year, we used to practise, our line—Toe Blake, Elmer Lach [of course, that is the famous Punch Line]—against Murph "Erwin" Chamberlain, Ray Getliffe and Phil Watson. They were on the other line and I used to score so many goals against them in practice. They started calling me the Rocket because I was scoring too many goals against them. The press was there, and some radio guys started calling me that.

From what I heard, during a practice a reporter named Dink Carroll of the *Montreal Gazette* overheard Ray Getliffe, a 10-year NHL veteran and left winger for the Canadiens, say, "Look at that new kid, he looks like a rocket." Maurice Richard from then on became Rocket Richard, and the greatest nickname in sports was born.

THE NIGHT THE ROCKET COULDN'T PLAY

WHEN WE SHOT THE *GRAPEVINE* SHOWS, the tape started recording and we didn't stop. It's called "live to tape" in the TV industry, and it means you just keep rolling and you don't stop and start over. The main reason we did it like this was because it's cheaper than stopping and starting and there is no editing.

But it means if I screwed up, it went to air. I couldn't say, "Oops, I made a mistake. Let's do it over." And if you make a mistake, everyone at home will see it. It happened during the Rocket's interview. As I said, Dick Beddoes and I were talking, before the Rocket came out, about the time he scored five goals in the playoffs and how the three stars were Richard, Richard and Richard.

For some reason, I got that game mixed up with the time the Rocket said he couldn't play. He corrected me, and everyone at home saw it. In many ways, it's a good thing—it makes the interview more natural.

> **DON:** Listen, those five goals you scored in the 5–1 game against the Leafs, I remember reading you told [coach] Dick Irvin that you wouldn't be able to play that night or something. You were tired.

> **ROCKET:** I don't think that was those five goals in the playoffs. It was five goals and three assists against Detroit in Montreal. That was the night I wasn't supposed to play.

DON: Why? What happened?

ROCKET: Well, I moved my family, all my furniture, with my brother in-law the night before the game and I didn't sleep all night, and I had only a few hours of rest before the game. I went to Mr. Dick Irvin before the game and said I wouldn't be able to play, I'm too tired. He said, "Oh, don't worry, you'll get some goals. It's an easy game." I went on and had eight or nine shots on net and had five goals and three assists.

DON: I guess you should have moved furniture every night.

* * *

One thing most people don't know is that Rocket was one of the first players to play right wing even though he was a left-hand shot. Nowadays, most guys play their off wing, but the Rocket was one of the first. I wondered how that got started.

DON: Now, you played right wing and you were a left-handed shot. You were one of the first. Why did you play right wing if you were a left-hand shot?

ROCKET: When I was playing junior, I was playing left wing and I always had a hard time turning on the defenceman on the left side. In my first year with the Canadiens, I asked the coach, Dick Irvin, if I could play right wing because it was easier for me to go around the defenceman from the right side, or going into the corner and coming back out in front was more natural for me.

DON: You can cut around the corner easier.

ROCKET: I used to cut around the net and it was easier for me. That's why you see a lot of guys today play on their off wing.

DON: You get to shoot at the whole net, too.

ROCKET: That's another thing. If you're right-handed and play right wing, you have more of a chance to use a backhand. If you're left-handed playing right wing, you have more chance to shoot forehand, and the angle is wider and you have more of a chance to hit the net.

DON: Yeah, you don't see too many guys shoot backhands now.

ROCKET: Well, you see a few, but it's pretty hard with that curved stick.

Playing on the off wing doesn't sound like a big deal today. Some of today's top scorers, like Alexander Ovechkin and Patrick Kane, play on their off wing, but the Rocket was the first to do it.

A SLOW START FOR THE ROCKET, AND DONNIE MARCOTTE

As you know, I go to a lot of minor midget games with my son, Tim. At the start of the season, it's really sad to see some kids on crutches or with their arm in a sling. They have gotten injured during the summer and they are so heartbroken at not being able to play. Sometimes I go over and talk to them, trying to give them a pep talk, but most times it's like the end of the world to them. It's something all players have to play through at some point in their career. The Rocket was no exception.

DON: You really had some serious injuries early in your career. Everybody was saying you had brittle bones.

ROCKET: I wasn't sure if I was going to play hockey after my first two years with the Canadiens senior group. First year with the Montreal Seniors, I had a broken ankle and a broken wrist. Then my first year with Canadiens in the NHL, I had another broken ankle. So in three years of hockey, I only played about 20 games, that's all.

It was a tough start for the Rocket, but he got through it.

DON: But then you went on—

ROCKET: After that, I went on to play 14 seasons without any real injuries.

* * *

For the past while, the NHL has put in a lot of rules to help get the scoring up. Most of the rules make it harder for players to check the superstars. A little hook or slash is now a penalty. Checking was tough when I coached the Bruins. You could interfere more and you could get away with some harder checks. When the Rocket played, it was unreal—you could do pretty much anything you wanted to try and stop him.

DON: I used to go and see some of your games. When I think of guys checking today, I remember you cutting over the blue line one time, and you actually had a guy on top of your back. That's the way they used to check.

Then the Rocket surprised me. He asked me a question.

ROCKET: What do you think you would have done when you were coaching the Bruins and I was playing against your team?

DON: I would have had Don Marcotte right on your back.

Don Marcotte played for me all five years in Boston. He was a left winger who was one of the greatest checkers ever in the NHL. There are a lot of unjust things in the NHL, and Don not winning the Selke Trophy for best defensive player ranks right up there.

When we played Montreal, he was on the ice at all times when Guy Lafleur was on the ice. That's how we got the too-many-men penalty in Game 7 of the '79 semifinals. We were up by a goal late in Game 7 in the Forum, Scotty Bowman was triple-shifting Guy, and Don was on his back the whole time.

Because Don was on the ice so long with Guy, our left wingers got confused about which player was up for the next shift. When Don finally came to the bench, I still remember walking over to him and patting him on the back, saying, "Way to go," and he looked up and said, "Oh, no." I knew what was happening the second he said, "Oh, no."

Two of our left wingers jumped on the ice, and we got the penalty for too many men on the ice. The Canadiens went on to tie the game—Guy scored on that power play—and went on to win in overtime. That was my last game as the Bruins' coach.

Marcotte wasn't just a checker, either. He scored 20 or more goals every year, except in '75–76, when he had an injury.

It's a crime he didn't get recognized as one of the best defensive players in the game. So when the Rocket asked me who I would have had checking him, I thought of nobody better than Don Marcotte.

* * *

In the Rocket's day, stars couldn't complain about their treatment. They just had to battle through it, which is why he had over 1,200 penalty minutes in his career.

ROCKET: I enjoyed playing that way because every time a man was following me, it made me work harder, fired me up and made me work harder. It's a good thing I had someone checking me for 14 years.

DON'T FOOL WITH THE ROCKET

WE INTERVIEWED *HOCKEY NIGHT IN CANADA*'s Dick Irvin Jr., whose father (Dick Irvin Sr.) coached the Rocket from 1942 until 1955. Dick Jr. watched the Rocket up close for most of his career.

DON: Just how tough was the Rocket?

DICK JR.: When people ask who is the greatest this or the greatest that, people forget Maurice Richard. He was one of the greatest fighters in the history of hockey. He knocked out four players. Bob "Killer" Dill [played for the Rangers from '43 to '45], he got him twice in one game. Once on the ice and once in the penalty box. He knocks him out on the ice; they go into the penalty box. Now Dill is upset because his image is tarnished—he just came up from the minors—so he took him on in the penalty box and Rocket got him again.

Then the Rocket fought the Hawks' John Mariucci. They fought on the ice, and then they fought in the penalty box. Then the Rocket fought the Rangers' Bill Juzda—a fierce battle with sticks and fists.

The Rocket also fought the Wings' Ted Lindsay. There was a big playoff series against Detroit in 1952. The Wings had finished 35 points ahead of the Canadiens. In the fifth game in Detroit, the Red Wings are leading and things aren't going too good [for Montreal], and Rocket flattened Lindsay. Montreal went on to win the series. My dad had headlines underlined in the paper: ROCKET'S PUNCH TURNS SERIES AROUND. My dad loved that stuff.

THE RICHARD RIOTS

JUST HOW LOVED WAS THE ROCKET in Montreal? When then NHL president Clarence Campbell suspended the Rocket for the last three games of the season and the playoffs, the fans in Montreal rioted. I didn't know how the Rocket would take being asked about it, but you had to ask.

DON: Now, I know Hal Laycoe wasn't one of your favourites when you played.

ROCKET: Don't talk about Hal Laycoe.

DON: I remember in the paper you had a big cut on your head, too. Quickly tell us what happened.

ROCKET: Well, quickly, Laycoe hit me over the head [with his stick], the play kept going and I came back at him and tried swinging at him, not with the stick. That's when I saw the blood. I had a guy, a linesman named [Cliff] Thompson, holding me from behind. Three times I had to try and get rid of him. The third time, I turned around and hit the linesman.

DON: You got fined $2,500, a $1,000 peace bond, and Mr. Campbell suspended you for the rest of the season and the playoffs.

ROCKET: There were only three games left in the season, but I think the playoffs were a bad suspension. I think I should have been suspended for the following season.

After the fight with Laycoe, Clarence Campbell had a hearing and decided to suspend the Rocket for the three games and the whole playoffs. It was the second time the Rocket was in trouble with Mr. Campbell that season. The suspension was the longest and harshest in his 31 years as NHL president. Campbell sent out a 1,200-word press release explaining his decision.

> *Assistance can also be obtained from an incident that occurred less than three months ago in which the pattern of conduct of Richard was almost identical, including his constant resort to the recovery of his stick to pursue his opponent, as well as flouting the authority of and striking officials. On the previous occasion he was fortunate that teammates and officials were more effective in preventing him from doing injury to anyone and the penalty was more lenient in consequence. At the time he was warned there must be no further incident . . . The time for probation or leniency is past. Whether this type of conduct is the product of temperamental instability or willful defiance of the authority in the games does not matter. It is a type of conduct which cannot be tolerated by any player—star or otherwise. Richard will be suspended from all games both league and playoff for the balance of the current season.*

DON: That's what they did back then, they suspended you from the playoffs. The riot after you got suspended was really something.

ROCKET: The riot, I didn't like it, no doubt about that. When I went into the Forum that night, we were playing against the Detroit Red Wings. I went to sit right behind the goalie. It was after the first period, somebody threw a bomb and it was right beside Mr. Campbell. Mr. Campbell went into the medical room, and I tried to go and talk to Mr. Campbell, but I was with the head of the Montreal police. He grabbed me and said, "Never mind. Don't talk to him."

DON: Then the fans went out and rioted.

I'll go into a little more detail on the riot. It was St. Patrick's Day, 1955. The game was for first place, and Montreal was getting hammered 2–0 halfway through the first period when Mr. Campbell took his seat.

You had to ask why Mr. Campbell would go to the game knowing the feeling in Montreal at the time. I guess he wanted to show everyone that he was not afraid and he was justified in giving the Rocket a harsh suspension.

At the end of the first period, it was 4–1 for the Wings, so the Montreal crowd was not in a good mood. Police and security were keeping people away from Mr. Campbell, but things were being thrown at him. Someone slipped through the police and went to shake Mr. Campbell's hand, but when he stuck out his hand, the man slapped Mr. Campbell.

All hell broke loose, and then someone threw the smoke bomb the Rocket mentioned. The angry crowd spilled out of the Forum and onto Sainte-Catherine Street. They say the riot covered 15 square blocks, some 12 policemen were injured, and it went well into the night.

ROCKET: I didn't see the riot because I had to stay in the Forum, in the medical room.

DON: You had to go on the radio and tell them to stop, just like the Pope.

ROCKET: I went on the radio the next morning. I told the people I was taking the blame and I was going to take the punishment and asked them to stop, and everything was quiet after that.

The Rocket went on the radio and TV and read this statement:

Because I always try so hard to win and had my troubles in Boston, I was suspended. At playoff time it hurts not be in the game with the boys. However, I want to do what is good for the people of Montreal and the team. So that no further harm will be done, I would like to ask everyone to get behind the team and to help the boys win from the Rangers and Detroit. I will take my punishment and come back next year to help the club and the younger players to win the Cup.

The riot stopped, but almost $100,000 in damage was done. That's about $1,000,000 in today's money.

* * *

Dick Beddoes, the second guest that night and a great sports reporter who was on CHCH-TV, asked a great question later in the show.

DICK: Rocket, did you ever make up with Clarence Campbell before he died with respect to that incident in 1955?

ROCKET: No doubt. I went to see him in the hospital once, just before he died. There is no doubt that President Campbell was a good friend of mine and he always spoke well about Rocket Richard. But I'm still mad at him because he suspended me for the playoffs.

THE ROCKET ON THE GREAT ONE

THERE IS ALWAYS THE AGE-OLD QUESTION: How would one superstar do in another era? Someone asked me how Bobby Orr would do in today's hockey. It's scary to think how many points he'd score.

DON: How do you think Gretzky would have done playing in your era?

ROCKET: Well, no doubt that Wayne would score goals — maybe not as many as right now and not as many points, but he'd still lead the league, no doubt. He's a natural and he's hard to beat. If he doesn't get any injuries [remember, this was 1984], he will set all new records in the league. I'd love to have played with him, that is for sure.

HOW THE ROCKET GOT THE NUMBER 9, AND THE LAST TIME I SAW THE ROCKET

THE ROCKET, GORDIE HOWE, BOBBY HULL. They all have one thing in common: they wore number 9. Gretzky wanted to wear number 9 in junior, but that number was taken, so he wore 99. But the Rocket was the first superstar to wear that number.

DON: All the greats wore 9, and you were the first. How did you get the number 9?

ROCKET: That was a long time ago. The second year I was with the Canadiens, my wife was going to have a baby and I was playing an exhibition game in Cornwall. After the game, I got a phone call, and my wife had a baby girl who weighed nine pounds. Before that, Dick Irvin told me to tell him how much the baby weighed when she was born. He said, "Your baby weighed nine pounds, so I'm going to give you the number 9." Charlie Sands was 9 when he played for the Canadiens, but he didn't stay for training camp that year. And that's how I got the number 9.

So if his baby had weighed eight pounds, all the greats would have worn number 8, and Gretzky would have been 88.

* * *

The last time I saw the Rocket was at his funeral in 2000. Ron and I were in the playoffs and we were doing the Philly–New Jersey series. The funeral was May 31 at the Notre-Dame Basilica, and we drove up to Montreal. In the days leading up to the service, over 150,000 fans paid their respects at the Molson Centre.

I wasn't sure if we should go. Sometimes, I feel like it's a grandstand play if I go to events like this. The other reason was I was not very popular in Quebec at that time.

Two years earlier, I got into trouble during the Olympics. Jean-Luc Brassard was named to be the Canadian flag bearer, and he said he didn't know if he wanted to carry the flag. Then Suzanne Tremblay, an MP with the Bloc Québécois, said she didn't like all the Canadian flags the Canadian athletes were flying at the athletes' village.

I went back on TV and said, "They don't like the Canadian flag, but they want our money and we bail them out. I've never seen such a bunch of whiners in all my life."

Suzanne Tremblay stood up in Parliament and said the usual stuff about me. The last thing I wanted to do was cause a big ruckus at the Rocket's funeral. But it was the Rocket, and I wanted to pay my respects.

As Ron and I were walking up the stairs of the Notre-Dame Basilica, a woman came up behind me and grabbed my arm.

She said, "Donnie, I know the Rocket would be glad you came."

I didn't see her, and I asked Ron who it was. He said, "Suzanne Tremblay." Now, with MacLean, I don't know if he was setting me up or not, so I'm still not sure who it was.

It was a state funeral, and I remember seeing a headline in the New York Times saying, MAURICE RICHARD'S FUNERAL BRINGS

*Smokin' Joe landing a big left hook on Ali during their first fight
in Madison Square Garden, March 1971.*

*Gerry Patterson, Tim and me.
One of the few times Gerry's not laughing.*

From left to right: Cindy, Bobby, Rose, me and Tim at the end of the Grapevine show in Hamilton.

In his last full year playing for me in Boston,
Bobby had 46 goals, 89 assists, 135 points, plus 128, and had over 100 minutes in penalties.
The only defenceman ever to lead the league in scoring.

The Rocket and Boom Boom Geoffrion celebrate after scoring a goal against the Leafs.
The Rocket lost his only chance of winning a scoring title to Boom Boom after he was
suspended for the last 3 games and the playoffs for punching a linesman.

This was the riot between Hal Laycoe and the Rocket. Laycoe (at the left of the shot) is held back by the linesman and Montreal's Bert Olmstead. The Rocket is along the boards and #8 Boston's Fleming Mackell (that spot on his sweater to the right of his number is Laycoe's blood) is trying to get to the Rocket. A short time later the Rocket punched the other linesman and got suspended for the rest of the season. Notice the photographer must have jumped on the ice to get this shot.

Wayne and Walter at Wayne's last game.

On the show, Ron Luciano told the story of how he blew this call at Yankee Stadium. That's Lou Piniella on the left, who was safe by a mile at home plate but called out by Ron, and #10 is Chris Chambliss giving it to Ron.

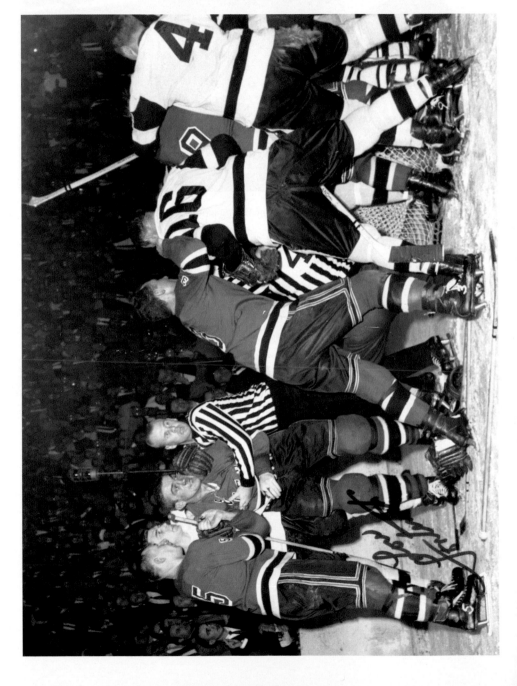

The brawling aftermath of Gordie Howe's fight with Lou Fontinato in the 1950s. Lou's on the left being held by the linesman and Gordie's in there somewhere. At the time, it was such a famous fight that the story of the battle made it into Life magazine.

World snooker champion Cliff Thorburn in 1987. They call him the grinder.

Everybody knows Red Storey as a ref, but he was also a Grey Cup hero.

Hard-rock defenceman Bobby Baun and I first met on the ice in my rookie year in Hershey. (Bobby didn't get caught by the ref for this.)

CANADA TO A STANDSTILL. It seemed like the country did pause, and rightly so.

There were over 2,500 people in the church and another 1,500 watching the service on a giant screen outside the church. It was also broadcast across the country.

As his brother Henri and other teammates started to carry the Rocket's casket out of the Basilica, Cardinal Jean-Claude Turcotte, the Archbishop of Montreal, said, "Let's give Rocket a hockey cheer like they used to in the Forum."

As the casket went down the aisle, the whole crowd cheered, "Vive le Rocket" over and over again.

I'm sure the Rocket would have approved.

The Rocket was a great guy while on the *Grapevine* show. He signed autographs for everybody, and like I said I can still remember those fiery eyes saying, "Don't fool with me."

RON LUCIANO

MLB umpire Ron Luciano, the easiest interview ever.
Just ask him one question and away he went with great stories.

RON AND THE YANKEES, AND THE LUCIANO CURSE

Like I said before, Tim and I wanted to go over all the questions with the guests before each show. We realized that the show was at its best when the guests told stories. I hate watching interviews when the host asks a 20-minute-long question.

We knew that our guests were athletes, not television professionals, and were not used to being in a sit-down, 15-minute-long interview situation. Plus, they were being interviewed in front of a live audience. Funny to see guys who played in front of 20,000 screaming fans terrified of being interviewed in front of 50 people. We wanted the guests to tell stories, not just give answers. So we thought if we told the guests the questions an hour before the taping, they could think about a story. It made for a better show.

One night, things got mucked up.

About five years into the show, Gerry Patterson, one of the executive producers, hired someone to help run his company. One day, he came to a taping of the show with his new business partner, I thought just to watch—not stick his nose in the production of the show. On this particular show, we had a non-hockey guest. When we had hockey players as guests, I would have about 10 to 15 questions. If I ran out of questions, I could throw in a couple of my own stories to fill out the time.

This night, our guest was not a hockey player, and I was not too familiar with the sport he played, so I had almost 30 questions prepared. Tim went over the questions and told the guest to think of stories, and that we weren't going to get to all the questions. I saw Gerry and his business partner talking to the guest right before the show, but I didn't think much of it.

I started off the interview.

DON: Where were you born?

GUEST: Toronto.

DON: When did you start curling?

GUEST: Ten.

DON: When you were young, how much did you practise?

GUEST: A lot.

DON: Who helped you out at that age?

GUEST: My dad.

The interview went on like this, with one-word answers. I went through all 30 questions in 10 minutes. I looked to my floor manager, Tommy Knight, to see how much time was left. He held up a sign: 15 MINUTES TO GO. I was stumbling and trying to think of curling questions on the fly. I threw to a commercial, and we still had half the show to do. Luckily, we had a hockey player as the next guest, and I asked him a bunch of questions to fill out the rest of the time. I couldn't figure out what had happened. It wasn't till later that we found out. Unbeknownst to Tim and me, Gerry's new business partner went to the guest and told him to keep his answers short and to the point. That was the last time he came to a taping of a show.

* * *

One guest that wasn't like that was major league baseball umpire Ron Luciano.

On October 14, 1985, we had Ron on to promote his second book, *Strike Two*. Ron was a great guest, and we had him on a few times. When word got out that Ron was coming on the show, we'd get a lineup of people wanting to come and be in the audience. This time, Ron brought his mother and sister to the show; it was a real Luciano family affair.

Tim sat down with Ron before the show to go over the questions.

Ron would ask, "How long do we have?" Tim would tell him 15 minutes, and he'd say, "OK, ask me about Billy Martin, Nolan Ryan and Jim McKean. That should be good."

So when the show started taping, I'd say, "OK, Ron, what about you and Billy Martin?"

He'd go off on a couple of stories and have the audience rolling on the floor. Easiest and one of the best interviews ever.

We always had a video-highlight clip of the guests, and we called them Blue Movies after my lovely bull terrier, Blue. One of the clips we showed of Ron was a play between the New York Yankees and the Milwaukee Brewers. The highlight showed Ron calling home plate. There were two out, Yankees down by one, with Yankees outfielder Lou Piniella on third. There was a line drive to centre; Lou had to hold up to see if the ball was going to be caught by Milwaukee's centre fielder. The ball dropped in for a hit and Lou took off for home, the centre fielder picked up the ball on one hop and threw a frozen rope to home. It wasn't even a close call at home plate, and Lou was safe — but Ron called Piniella out. The video showed the Yankees going nuts screaming and yelling at Ron. Check out the photograph of that play in the photo insert.

DON: Why do they always boo umpires?

RON: I don't know why. I have a mother and a father.

DON: Boy, the Yankees really gave it to you on the video.

RON: They loved it, they loved the call. Did you see Piniella rolling around on the ground? He should have gotten an Oscar. Number 10, Chris Chambliss, who was with the Yankees at the time and was one of the nicest guys, seeing him jumping up and down — I think I might have made an error. Chambliss, who never said anything to me my whole career, started to cry. When the tears started to come down his face, I thought maybe I did make a mistake. Then third baseman Graig Nettles, one of the nicest guys in the whole world, looked at me and said, "You no good *bleep, bleep, bleep.*" Then I said to myself, "I know I made a mistake."

* * *

When Ron walked on to the set, I couldn't get over how big he was. He was at least six foot four and over 250 pounds. He must have been intimidating in his prime.

DON: You used to play college football.

RON: I played for Syracuse University the year before they became the number one champs in the U.S.

DON: The year before?

RON: Yes, the year *before*. If I would have stayed, well, who knows. Then I left and played football with the Detroit Lions. In the '50s, the Lions won three NFL championships. I was drafted by them, and they've never won since. Then I left and went to Buffalo—even with O.J. [Simpson] they never won. They couldn't win, and they blamed it on me. So then I then went to Al Summers Umpire School, and the next year it went bankrupt. I then joined the American baseball league. I was there for 12 years. Just take a wild guess how many All-Star games they [the American League] lost in a row: 12. I wrote a book, the day after the printers shipped out the copies, the printers burned to the ground. I'm not kidding you. I did a commercial for Gulf Oil of Canada. Guess what? No more Gulf Oil of Canada. I got rid of them.

DON: So does that mean . . .

RON: Sorry, Don, this is your last show.

The funny thing is, he was right. He was the last guest of the year for us.

RON'S LIFE IN THE MINORS

JUST LIKE ATHLETES, ALL UMPIRES—AND REFS, for that matter—start off in the minor leagues. Life for umps is no better than life for players in the minors.

DON: I love your book.

RON: Come on, you can't read. I talked to all the NHL refs and they said you can't read, but boy, could you swear.

DON: Rose read it to me and I looked at all the pictures. Now, in the minors, that must have been something, umpiring in those small towns.

RON: In the minor leagues, they taught you things. Like never leave any clothes in the dressing room [see, Ron was old school: it's a dressing room, not a locker room!], because they are not going to be there when you get back. Not because someone is going to steal them. The animals and the insects would eat 'em up. It's so bad. The $100,000 ballplayers, well, they were dressing in luxury. You should see where we dressed. One time, there was water dripping down—we didn't know where it was coming from. It was the bathroom in the stadium. I spent five years in the minors and I wanted to get out of there so quick. We'd try and climb over each other. I'd read the paper, the obituaries, to see which umpires died upstairs so I could move up.

DON: I read that in your book. Is that true?

RON: Yes, it's a dog-eat-dog game, even for umpires. When I was in the league, there were only 52 umpires in the league in the States and Canada. Well, we have one Canadian token. Jim McKean was in the league four years, and never had a close call. No matter where he was, it was never close. If it was a close play at first, he was at third. Guy steals into second, he's at home. He's never anyplace it was close. He was always saying, "What's tough? This is easy." Nobody swore at him. Nobody called his mother names. For four years. Then, Opening Day in Milwaukee. We're in the bottom of the ninth inning. The New York Yankees are ahead, 7–4. We got the bases loaded. Up at bat is Don Money. Of course it's a close ball game, and where is McKean? First base. There is no way he's going to be at home — there's too much trouble there, right? The Yankees' first baseman at the time was Chris Chambliss. He wants a time-out. McKean says, "You want time?" Yankee pitcher winds up, throws the ball. Home run! A grand slam! Milwaukee goes on to win, 8–7, everybody goes nuts. The crowd is going crazy, the players run off the field and into the dugout. And McKean says, "Excuse me, umm, I had time-out. Doesn't count. You gotta bring everybody back." The poor guy. He was shell shocked.

* * *

For all the things Ron was known for, he was most famous for "shooting" players when he called them out. He would make a "gun" with his thumb and forefinger. When it was a close play and the player was out, he'd "shoot" them four or six times. The more Ron did this, the more fans loved it. Fans would go to games to see him "shoot" players after a strikeout or a close play at first.

DON: When did you start shooting guys?

RON: It was in Kansas City. There was a player named Amos Otis, a centre fielder for the Royals, and I really liked the guy a lot. Every time he came up to bat, I'd call him out, no matter what it was. Strike one — you're out. He'd say, "Geez, give me two more." They said it was a mental block, but we know that's not true because us umpires don't have any-thing mental — nothing upstairs. He'd steal second and the catcher wouldn't even throw the ball to second, and I'd yell,

"You're out!" He'd look up and say, "Give me a chance." One year, all winter long, I practised "Amos is safe, Amos is safe, Amos is safe." I wrote it down on a piece of paper. And it worked. The next season, he was batting and I was behind the plate. The pitcher threw the ball and I said, "Strike one—you're safe." Amos looked at me and said, "Safe on one strike?" He'd slide into first and was out by twenty feet. I'd yell, "Safe!" The next game, Kansas's manager came up to me before the game and said, "What is Amos going to be today? Is he going to be safe or out? Because if he's out, I'm not going to be playing him."

I went to the other umpires and asked, "What am I doing wrong? Am I looking at the girls in the stands too much, or am I calling too quick? What am I doing wrong?" They told me, "Just relax." So I'm at first base and Amos hits one right back to the mound. I know he's going to be out by a mile. So I run down—well, I don't run, I waddle down, right to first base—and yell, "I got ya! I got ya!" [While Ron's saying this, he has his fingers in the "gun" pose.] The dugout started yelling, "Shoot him! Shoot him!" So I said, "You're out," and yelled, "Bang! Bang! Bang!" The crowd went nuts, and from then on it was no more mundane outs.

I was in the stands one day in Cleveland. Well, Cleveland, that's where elephants go to die. There were three or four people in the stands—a typical crowd for Cleveland. I was at first base and I missed about six plays in the first six innings, so I said that's it, I could do it better from the stands. So I sat in the stands for the seventh, eighth and ninth inning. I got a standing ovation. Ball hit to the shortstop, he'd throw it to first, I'd be in the stands, yelling, "Hey kid, you're out!" The fans would cheer and yell at me, "Hey, great, you got one right!" So looking back, in the stands, I was great. It was when I was on the field that I was bad.

RON AND BILLY MARTIN

ONE OF MY FAVOURITE MANAGERS OF all time was the Yankees' Billy Martin. He and Ron had some legendary run-ins.

> **DON:** Billy Martin. Tell us about Billy.

> **RON:** I love Billy Martin. Billy used to do things like run up to me in the middle of the game and start yelling, "I'll tell you one thing, I got a hangover!" I'd look at him and say, "A hangover?" Billy would go on and say, "Yeah, and I'm getting the crowd on you, aren't I?" The crowd would be going nuts, yelling at me. Billy would say, "My head's about to bust. I'm going into the dugout and letting [team owner George] Steinbrenner know what a good job I did yelling at ya." And then he'd run back into the dugout.

Funny, I had the same thing happen to me, except it was the ref getting the fans on the coach's back. I was with Boston and we were in Toronto, and the game was on *Hockey Night in Canada*. I'd been yelling at ref Dave Newell, giving him a hard time about something.

We'd just come out of a commercial break and the puck was about to be dropped. Dave blew his whistle and skated right over to our bench. I went to the door, ready to have it out with him.

He skated right up and got right in my face and pointed his finger at my chest and said, "Grapes, that's the sharpest suit I've seen you wear this year." The crowd went nuts. They were cheering and yelling at Dave, saying, "Way to give it to him, ref! Don't take any crap from Cherry."

I was stunned. I didn't know what to say.

I learned later that *Hockey Night in Canada* was broadcasting a shot of him and me, and Bob Cole was saying, "Dave Newell is severely reprimanding Don Cherry."

Then Dave started to point at my tie and say, "I love that tie. It goes great with that suit."

This got the crowd into a frenzy. He skated away and quickly turned around and yelled out really loud, "And don't you forget it!" The Gardens was going crazy. For the first time, I didn't know what to say. The players on both benches were killing themselves laughing.

I pulled that joke on Ron MacLean one year, and it kind of backfired on me. It was in the 2006 Stanley Cup finals between Edmonton and Carolina. All season long, there was a lot of controversy about the new rules in the NHL. That was the year that if you shot the puck over the glass, it was an automatic penalty. That one drove me nuts. But the biggie was calling all the little hooking and holding and generally calling a lot more penalties. It was a great final and everything was going well, and then my joke on Ron kind of went off the rails.

Ron interviewed Colin Campbell—who at that time was the NHL's senior vice-president and director of hockey operations— between the second and third periods of Game 4 of the finals. He kind of gave Colin a hard time on some of the rule changes.

As usual, after the interview, Ron felt a little bad that he gave Colin such a hard time. The next day, we were in the Edmonton airport, waiting for a flight to Carolina. I was kidding Ron about how hard he had been on Colin, and it was starting to get to him. We were waiting to board, and in the boarding lounge were all the *Hockey Night in Canada* crew, the NHL officials and a lot of the press covering the finals.

As we were waiting to board, I saw Stephen Walkom, who at the time was vice-president and director of officiating of the NHL and a good friend of Ron's.

I said to Ron, "There's Walkom, and I'm going over and giving him hell about all these rules and I'm going to tell him that you agree with me."

Ron shook his head no and said, "Just leave it alone."

I said, "No I'm going to tell him that you and I hate these new rules," and I stormed off towards Stephen, who was at the other end of the lounge.

I went up to Stephen and said, "Look, I'm going to pretend to give you hell and I'm going to point at Ron. You give him a really dirty look."

So I pretended to be giving Stephen hell. I yelled loudly, "Stupid rule!" and then pointed to Ron. Stephen kept a pretty good straight face and gave Ron a real dirty look. Ron just about melted. I kept it up for about 30 seconds and stormed off.

Stephen played it to a T, and Ron was really mad at me. But then the joke turned on me. A few days later—June 14, 2006, to be exact—I looked at the morning *Toronto Star*. In the sports section, the headline read, NEW ICE AGE KILLING OFF NHL'S DINOSAURS: CHERRY TAKES RUN AT OFFICIATING CHIEF. I guess a reporter for the *Star* saw my little joke and fell for it too. The article in the *Star* went on to say:

The scene was Edmonton International Airport, an unlikely place for a symbolic clash between the old NHL and the new.

Don Cherry, the populist voice for those who yearn for the dismissed days of scrums, scraps and unregulated hand-to-hand combat on ice, barked his disfavour. "Stupid rule," he said loudly as passengers boarding an Air Canada flight yesterday morning for Toronto craned their necks to learn the target of Cherry's un-mistakable thundering. That target, although those marvelling at Cherry's celebrity might have been unable to identify him, was league refereeing commander Stephen Walkom. Cherry's ire had been stirred once more by the new rule that prohibits defending players from rifling the puck over the glass in their own zone to kill play and thereby dissolve troublesome opposition advances. It's a rule that has been called only occasionally in these out-standing Stanley Cup playoffs, but it is one that has become the central focus of Cherry's disdain for all the NHL rule changes and altered standards that he despises but has been utterly power-less to block or overturn despite his extensive popularity and influence in Canadian hockey circles. Walkom, knowing his boss, Gary Bettman, has already thrown his support solidly behind the over-the-glass rule, simply smiled and joined his colleagues.

Stephen walked over to his colleagues and smiled because he and I were the only ones in on the joke. But the joke was on me because I was once again called a dinosaur by the *Toronto Star*. That's OK. I've been called worse.

SOUNDS LOW, MANAGING THE GAME AND EARL WEAVER

Ron Luciano told a lot of great stories, but this was my favourite.

DON: Tell us about Nolan Ryan.

RON: I was behind the plate when Nolan got his second no-hitter in 1973, I think. The first time I called balls and strikes when he was pitching was crazy. I was thinking, "OK, how hard can this guy really throw?" I was watching him warm up and said to myself, "Yeah, he can really throw hard." I get behind the plate and he winds up, and then I hear a pop. It's in the catcher's glove. Didn't see a thing. Didn't see it leave his hand, didn't see it cross the plate, didn't see anything. Now the catcher looks at me for the call. The batter is looking at me for the call. I hesitate and say, "Ball—sounds low."

The crowd just roared when he told the story. In one of Ron's books, *The Umpire Strikes Back,* he talks about calling more strikes when the game was a blowout and he was trying to get the game over with. He joked about wanting to have dinner early. But I know, and the players know, why he did that. What he was doing was managing the game. A lot of so-called pundits of the game would say that is wrong. The pundits say a strike is a strike no matter what the score of the game or what the count on the batter is.

What Ron was trying to avoid was someone on the winning team sliding hard into second or someone admiring a home run. If that happened, Ron knew what would be coming next: balls would be fired at batters' heads. He knew baseball and the mentality of the players. To be a good ref or umpire, you have to know that part of the game. It's something you can't teach. You either have the knack or you don't.

Hockey refs used to manage the game back when I played and coached, but they don't so much now. When I was with the Bruins and we'd be up by a lot of goals, we knew we were going to get the next few penalties. It helped keep the game under control.

We were up by a few goals in Washington one game, and John McCauley, maybe the greatest ref of all time, gave us about four penalties in a row.

After we killed off the fourth penalty, I said, "OK, John, is that enough?" He nodded his head. "Yeah, Grapes, that's enough."

He was managing the game. He knew Washington was embarrassed and didn't want them to start running around and trying to start trouble, which he knew the Bruins would finish. He stopped things from happening instead of giving penalties after trouble started. If you think that sounds easy, you're wrong. You have to have a feel for the game and the players. If you don't have a feel for the game and you don't know what you're doing, you can get into trouble trying to manage a game.

I was at a minor midget playoff game last year. It was between a Mississauga team and a Toronto team, and these two teams had a lot of bad blood between them throughout the whole season. The Mississauga team got up four goals fairly early in the game, and as the game wound down in the third period, it started to get vicious. You couldn't believe the stickwork. They didn't fight, but they were sticking each other pretty good. The ref started to call a lot of penalties, I think to try and control the game, but he kept calling them on the Toronto team that was losing big. All this did was get Toronto more frustrated. Mississauga would score and rub it in a bit on the Toronto team.

Next faceoff, the Toronto team would start up again. Emotions on both sides were running high and they were spearing and slew-footing each other. The ref kept calling penalties on the Toronto team and things kept escalating. Players were thrown out of the game, got into their suits and ties and started yelling at each other from off the ice. The coaches were yelling at each other. It was a hair's breadth away from becoming an all-out riot.

Now, if John McCauley was calling this game, he would have kept calling penalties on the winning Mississauga team. This would have kept Toronto on the power play and kept them from running around, and there would have been no trouble.

To me, refereeing or umpiring a game is more than calling the rules, it's managing the game, which has become a lost art.

* * *

You can't talk to Ron and not ask about Earl Weaver. If you don't know, Earl Weaver was the small, fiery manager of the Baltimore Orioles from 1968 to 1982. People would pay money hoping that Earl would go on the field and have it out with an umpire. He was a fan favourite—he looked just like a little banty rooster arguing with umps.

I'll give you a little background on the battles that Ron and Earl fought. They started in the minors. Ron and Earl first met in Double-A ball. The legend goes that Earl was managing the Elmira Pioneers in 1965 and they were in a four-game series. Ron ejected Earl from all four games—the fourth time even before a pitch was thrown. When they both got to the majors, one day

Ron ejected Earl from both games of a doubleheader. The second time, he turfed Earl during the pre-game lineup exchange. Let's just say they didn't like each other.

When Ron was umpiring an Orioles game, it was worth the price of the tickets to see these two go at it.

> **DON:** Now how did you and Earl—

> **RON:** Why did you mention him? I was having such a good time . . . why did you have to ruin it? You know, the problem with Earl Weaver was he was too short [he was five foot seven and Ron was six foot four, so you can imagine they looked like Mutt and Jeff when they were going at it] and he never saw a parade. He was always in the second row and could never see. He was too short. I said I don't care who wins the World Series as long as Baltimore doesn't.

Then Ron got me good.

> **RON:** Earl and I hate each other, but we had dinner on Sunday.

I bit, hook, line and sinker.

> **DON:** Really?

> **RON:** Yeah, he was in Baltimore and I was in New York. That's as close as we've been in 10 years.

The audience just roared at that one. He got me good. Ron was one of the greatest guests. He was funny and the audience just loved him. After the show ended, he signed autographs and took pictures. He kept on telling stories well after the show had wrapped up, and the crowd hung on his every word. Ron's gone now, and baseball is the lesser for it.

BOBBY BAUN

Bobby having a good laugh recalling how he choked me during a fight in the AHL. I told the crowd, "He went to the NHL the next year and I stayed in the minors or I would have gotten him back."

THE FIRST TIME I MET BOBBY BAUN

ON SEPTEMBER 19, 1991, I INTERVIEWED HARD-ROCK DEFENCE-MAN Bobby Baun from Lanigan, Saskatchewan. In 1964 I was playing for the Rochester Americans of the AHL and we were the farm club of the Toronto Maple Leafs. Bobby had been with the Leafs for nine years. We had our training camp together in Peterborough, Ontario.

> **DON:** Now, I played for Rochester and we were at the Leafs camp. Do you remember me?
>
> **BOBBY:** We had a tough time forgetting about you.

One of the things Bobby Baun and I had in common was Punch Imlach. I played for Punch in Springfield under the Darth Vader of hockey, Eddie Shore. It was 1957, and at that time both Punch and I were far away from the NHL.

Punch said to me, "Don, I'm going to make it to the NHL, and you will, too."

I thought to myself, "Sure, Punch, you're going to make it to the NHL."

Four years later, Punch had not only made it to the NHL, he had won the Stanley Cup with the Leafs.

Seven years after Punch told me he was going to make it to the NHL, I was playing for the Rochester Americans. Punch was in his fourth year of coaching the Leafs, winning three Stanley Cups in a row. Punch was the toast of hockey.

In 1964, both the Leafs and Rochester held training camp in Peterborough. At that time, rookie Ron Ellis said he didn't know if he wanted to go to college or turn pro with the Leafs. Punch convinced him to play for the Leafs, and there was a big buzz about Ellis.

For some reason, Punch told the trainer to have me scrimmage with the big club. Punch was watching from the stands and, as Ellis was coming down the wing, he cut into centre.

I don't know if it was by habit or if I was pissed off about Ellis saying he didn't know if he wanted to play pro, but I stepped up and nailed him good.

Punch came running down the stands and yelled, "Get that 50-cent hockey player off the ice with my million-dollar player."

I smashed my stick over the boards and threw it to centre ice and skated off the rink.

I never really thought about it at that time, but looking back, I wonder if Punch was giving me a chance to make the Leafs.

DON: Do you remember when I hit Ellis?

BOBBY: He didn't know if he was Martha or Arthur after that hit.

DON: Do you remember the first time we met?

BOBBY: I can hardly wait for this.

I first saw Bobby Baun when he played with Al MacNeil. They were rock'em sock'em boys. Both could hit a ton, but neither were really good fighters. Bobby was with the Rochester Americans in 1956. I was playing for the Hershey Bears.

During a game against Bobby and the Amerks, a fight broke out. I was standing there, minding my own business, watching the fight, and Baun came up behind me, put his arm around my neck and started to choke me.

As I struggled to turn around, I fell and he fell on top of me. The rest of the players piled on top.

I was at the bottom of the pile, Baun choking me, and I couldn't breathe. The more I struggled, the tighter he choked me.

I thought, "This is how I'm going to die." Luckily, the other players got off us and the refs pulled us apart.

I do have to thank Bobby, because he taught me a lesson: always be ready on the ice. No one ever snuck up on me again.

When I told this story to the audience, Bobby was laughing.

BOBBY: Timmy [Horton] and I like to wrestle better than fight.

DON: You went up to the NHL and I spent 16 years in the minors, or I would have got you.

BOBBY: You just wanted to ride in the iron lung.

WHAT BOBBY BAUN AND SCOTT STEVENS HAD IN COMMON

YOU DON'T SEE TOO MANY OPEN-ICE hits in today's game. Bobby was known for being one of the hardest open-ice hitters in the

NHL. He was rock solid at five foot ten, 180 pounds. When he got you in the trolley tracks, you were a goner. But he had some help.

> **DON:** You and Al MacNeil really had something going. You should have seen these guys—you get someone in the trolley tracks and it was curtains.

> **BOBBY:** It was a lot of fun. If a guy was coming down the wing, Al would stand up a little bit and the guy would have to head into centre ice, and I'd coming across and nail him.

> **DON:** And gone-zo.

Scott Stevens, maybe hockey's hardest hitter of all, was the same way. He used that very same play. Whoever his partner was would stand up at the blue line and force the player to cut into centre and get into the trolley tracks. Even before the player would start to cut into centre, Stevens would be coming across centre with those Rocket Richard–like eyes on fire.

In the 2000 playoffs, Stevens was at his prime, nailing guys. In the second round of the playoffs, the New Jersey Devils were playing the Leafs and I remember Stevens really nailed both Kevyn Adams and Tie Domi at the blue line.

In the semifinals, the Devils faced the Philly Flyers. Stevens was still on a tear, like a great white shark looking for his next victim. In Game 2 of the series, the Flyers' Daymond Langkow was going down the left side. The textbook play that let Bobby Baun nail guys back in the '60s was played out.

As Langkow was going down the left side, Devils defenceman Brian Rafalski stood up at the blue line, forcing Langkow to cut into centre. Stevens was coming across and just drilled him. Langkow missed the next game.

The series was a real tong war and the Devils jumped out a 3–2 lead in games. Now, Eric Lindros, who was one of the best players in the NHL at the time, had missed the last 30-some games because of a concussion, and he decided to come back for Game 6.

I went on "Coach's Corner" and said there is no way he should be coming back. He might have been in shape physically, but he was not in game shape. I said it was a big mistake.

That game, Eric scored a goal and rang one off the post and the Flyers won 2–1 to force Game 7 back in Philly.

After the game, Ron MacLean was bugging me about being wrong. He said Eric returning was going to be the big story. I told Ron I didn't care. Eric shouldn't be playing with a pit bull like Stevens on the ice.

During the first period of Game 7, Ron and I were still arguing as we were getting ready for "Coach's Corner." I told him the Flyers were going to rue the day they let Eric play in this series.

Ron said, "The only way you are going to be proven right is if Eric comes down the left side and cuts into centre and Stevens corks him."

I said, "Right."

Twenty seconds later, Eric comes down the left side, Scott Niedermayer stands up at the blue line, forcing Eric towards the centre, and Stevens just drills him. Eric is out cold, he does a Spandau ballet, his helmet rides up and his head smashes the ice.

I can still see poor Eric being helped off the ice by Adam Burt and John LeClair.

On "Coach's Corner," I showed Langkow's and Eric's hits and talked about how they looked like a replay of each other.

Eric was never the same after that. That was the last game he played as a Flyer. He missed all the next season and then was traded to New York.

I hate to tell you I told you so, but I told you so.

BAUN ON THE LEAFS' GLORY DAYS AND PUNCH

BOBBY PLAYED FOR THE LEAFS IN their glory days. He and the Leafs won three Cups in a row in 1962, '63 and '64, and then another in '67.

DON: The Leafs had a great run in the early '60s.

BOBBY: We had a lot of fun with that Maple Leaf club. Just a great group of guys. We had 12 or 13 of the best crew from the late '50s to '67. A much older club. We had guys like Allan Stanley, Johnny Bower, Terry Sawchuk in the last years.

DON: Bert Olmstead was a big part.

BOBBY: Bert turned that whole team around at that time. He was a real leader. He forgot more about hockey than most guys knew.

DON: Tell us about my old coach Punch. I heard that Punch had worked the older players as hard, if not harder, than the younger players.

BOBBY: Everything was fair with Punch. He'd give you a shot even if you did something wrong. One of the great stories was I had a baby girl born while we were in Montreal, and I took all the boys to the Queen E. hotel for a party the night before we were to play the Montreal Canadiens. We even changed the baby's name from Mary to Michelle because we were in Quebec. Anyway, the next night we were playing Montreal in the Forum, and it was tied 4–4 in the third period and we were a little hungover. Henri Richard came down in the third period on Timmy Horton. Henri made a move on him, and Tim did about three pirouettes. Henri went in on Johnny Bower, gave him the old head shake and put it in the top corner — 5–4. By the end of the night, it was 9–4. Punch came into the dressing room and said, "I don't know what the hell you guys were up to last night, but it cost you $100." Michelle today is 27 [we did the interview in 1991]. That little baby cost me $2,700 plus my bar tab.

DON: I played for Punch in Springfield before he went to Toronto. You kinda hated the guy for the way he acted, but he was the best coach I ever played for by far.

BOBBY: I always said he wasn't as great a coach as he was a motivator, and he coached the same way that you did. I think you must have taken some lessons from him.

DON: Honest to God, he'd come into the dressing room with a hammer all the time and he'd have spikes in a table. He'd come in between periods, and if we were winning, he'd pound the nail and say, "That's one." You think grown men would, you know, but we really ate that stuff up. He really was a beauty.

Bobby was right when he called Punch a Knute Rockne of hockey.

BOBBY BAUN AND "THE GOAL"

WHEN YOU TALK ABOUT BOBBY BAUN, of course, you have to talk about *the goal*. Next to the one Bobby Orr scored flying through the air and Paul Henderson's goal against the Russians in '72, Baun's broken-ankle goal is the most famous goal in hockey history.

It was during Game 6 of the 1964 Stanley Cup finals against Gordie Howe and the Detroit Red Wings. The Leafs were down 3–2 in the series, facing elimination. It's the third period with the game tied.

DON: All right, tell us about the goal. Maybe one of the most famous goals in history.

BOBBY: I was running on emotion. . . . I'd gone into the dressing room with about 10 minutes to go in the game. I had gone into a faceoff with Gordie Howe [back then, defencemen took the draws in their own end of the ice], and I had just blocked a shot from Gordie previous to that. . . . I won the draw back and turned to go with Gordie, and I heard a bang and I fell to the ice and that was it. I went to the dressing room and asked the doctor if anything can be done. He said I could tape it [he didn't know it was broken at this time], so I asked if I could hurt it any more. The doctor said he didn't think so. He froze it for me and taped it. I went back out [the game was now in overtime] and Junior [Albert] Langlois committed the cardinal sin. In the left-hand corner, he threw the puck blindly around the boards and I hit a magnificent [of course he was joking] slapshot. Don, it was a triple flutter blaster, I called it. I could read "Art Ross" on the puck. It was going on the long side of Terry Sawchuk and it hit Bill Gadsby's stick. Bill, who I called Jinksy that whole series . . . hit his stick and went the opposite way on Terry and into the net.

It tied the series 3–3. The Leafs went on to win Game 7, 4–0, and the Stanley Cup.

THE DAY TIM HORTON SAVED BOBBY BAUN'S LIFE

OF COURSE, I COULDN'T TALK TO Bobby without asking about Tim Horton. Kinda sad to think a lot of Canadians don't even know who the doughnut shop is named after.

> **DON:** I remembered during a training camp [I was playing for Rochester], the players were around Tim Horton's big new car and asking what his next business adventure was, because he tried a hamburger place and failed.

> **BOBBY:** Yeah, he had trouble with the hamburger places. I loaned him $10,000 at the time for that business.

> **DON:** I remember hearing about something to do with a bakery and coffee place. Tim said something like, "Ya know when you just want to grab a quick coffee going to work? That's what I want to open." All the players laughed. Like I said, some of us hockey players aren't too bright. You said he saved your life one time in New York.

> **BOBBY:** I was coming out of the old Madison Square Garden on 49th Street, and there was a hospital nearby. On this particular night, I fell on Camille [The Eel] Henry's skate. It went underneath my throat right here [Bobby was pointing right underneath his chin]. This was in the middle of the second period. I had it stitched up and finished out the period. It was bothering me a little bit and I didn't play the third period, so by the time I got changed, I went out to the bus to wait for the guys. Tim usually ran down the road and had a beer at one of the local pubs after the game. By this time, my cut had hemorrhaged and it pushed my tongue back down my throat. I had gone off the bus and

passed out on 48th Street in New York City. Tim just luckily had come back [from the bar] and carried me into the St. Clare's Hospital. They had to do a tracheotomy at the time to relieve the pressure and get me breathing again.

How ironic that, at the time of the interview, Bobby owned a Tim Hortons franchise. You could sense some sadness when Bobby talked about how much Tim would have enjoyed all the trappings of a successful business like Tim Hortons.

> **DON:** If Tim could only see how things turned out for his dough-nut shop.

> **BOBBY:** Tim would have loved all the cars and jets that go with such a great company. Tim laughs at me every day. I got a big picture of Tim in the shop, over where I stand a lot of the time. I can see that big, stupid grin on him. He's upstairs, looking down at me, saying, "You little asshole."

Bobby worked just as hard at his Tim Hortons as he did on the ice. He was the first one to work in the morning making the dough-nuts, but fame is fleeting, as they say.

Let me explain.

It was the October 2006 opening game for the Leafs. That night, they were going to honour two numbers, numbers 4 and 21. I was in the "Coach's Corner" studio, watching the broadcast on a small monitor. I was kind of paying attention, but I was getting my thoughts ready for "Coach's Corner." I wait all summer to do the first "Coach's Corner," so I am usually pretty focused on what I'm going to talk about.

As I was watching the telecast, the ceremony started and they honoured Red Kelly and Hap Day, who wore number 4. Then they honoured number 21 and Börje Salming, which they should.

I went on to do something in the studio, and it hit me that Bobby Baun wore number 21 as well. Seventeen years in the NHL, a four-time Stanley Cup winner and scored maybe the most famous goal in Leafs history, and he wasn't even mentioned in the ceremony or on our telecast on *Hockey Night in Canada*.

I went on "Coach's Corner" and ripped the Leafs and *Hockey Night in Canada* for this glaring omission.

I received a letter from Bobby's wife, thanking me for mentioning him. He deserved to be recognized as a Stanley Cup winner. I was glad I was able to correct that mistake and have Bobby rightly acknowledged for his super years in the NHL and as a Leaf, even though he did try and choke me to death in Hershey.

GORDIE HOWE

Gordie showing me how short his stick was. I said, "It helped you get the stick up in player's faces quicker." He thought that was funny.

GORDIE HOWE AND COLD OPENINGS

ON OCTOBER 4, 1984, WE HAD GORDIE HOWE as our guest on the *Grapevine* show. Now, I was still pretty much a rookie as a TV personality. I'd only been doing "Coach's Corner" full time for about a year. Those segments were easier for me because I could just talk about hockey and I could jump from topic to topic. Plus, it only ran about eight minutes. We also shot "Coach's Corner" in a small set with only Dave Hodge, the cameraman and me.

The *Grapevine* was a different story. There was the double whammy: I had to memorize lines and read questions off a cue card. Not only that, we were taping in front of a live audience. They say the greatest fear in life is standing up and speaking in front of people. I had to do that with a TV camera in my face.

The hardest thing of all was the cold opening. I had to look into the camera and introduce that episode's guest. I was getting pretty good, and most of the time it only took a few takes. We shot the cold opening in a corner of the set in front of a big picture of Blue and me in the Bruins dressing room.

For this show, I had to say, "This week in the *Grapevine*, we have Hall of Famer Gordie Howe, Mr. Elbows. You ready? Let's go." Easy, right? I just couldn't say it. I kept screwing up. The more I screwed up, the more the audience would laugh, and that was throwing me off as well. I must have done it about 10 times.

Ralph Mellanby could see I was stuck and I could have been there all night. Ralph pulled me aside and said, "Just start off looking at the picture and then turn to the camera. Just say it to Blue and don't worry about doing it word for word." Ralph was right; I pretended to talk to Blue and the next take was a keeper.

But little did I know Gordie was hiding around the corner, and when I introduced him he came around the corner and gave me a shot with his elbow. The audience went nuts.

* * *

I always liked to see if the guest had any clue that we crossed paths in our hockey journeys.

DON: In 1961, I was at your training camp. Do you remember me?

GORDIE: Don, I hardly remember myself back then.

During my journey through the minors, I only remember really running into Gordie Howe once, and he actually spoke to me. You have to remember that back in those days, we minor leaguers were like ghosts to the guys in the NHL. They mostly looked right through us like we weren't even there.

It was at the Red Wings camp in 1961, and how I got there I have no idea. It was an early-morning practice, and I liked to be the first guy on the ice. I was slowly skating around the ice by myself. It was the first day of training camp, I was getting a feel for my equipment, and my jock didn't feel comfortable. I reached down my pants to adjust my jock.

As I was in the middle of my adjustment, Gordie came on the ice. He skated up behind me and said, "Having trouble finding it?"

You'd think I would have gotten mad. But you know what? I was just honoured that he said something to me.

* * *

Gordie's first pro season was in the USHL, with the Omaha Knights. His first season in the NHL was with, of course, the Wings in 1946–47. In today's NHL, first-year players are expecting to get a signing bonus. It's reported that Max Domi got a signing bonus of $277,500 in his first season with the Coyotes, and he's well worth it. But back when Gordie played, signing bonuses were not in the cards.

> **DON:** OK, now, Gretzky signs, he gets a yacht, a shopping centre and a car. What did you get?

GORDIE: I got a jacket.

> **DON:** That's all?

GORDIE: I'm very proud of that jacket.

> **DON:** I heard that you lived at the Olympia. Now, that's really loving hockey when you sleep there.

GORDIE: Yes, that was the first year and that was during the war. In Detroit there was really no place to stay. The first professional practice with the Detroit Red Wings, I was late. I was sleeping about 15 feet from the rink. I was in a little cubbyhole right across where the visitors use to dress. That's where I was sleeping and the noise on the boards woke me up and I ran down and got dressed in a hurry.

Yes, players do have it a little different today compared to back in Gordie's day.

WHY GORDIE LEFT HOCKEYTOWN, USA, AND BAUN SETS GORDIE STRAIGHT

WHEN YOU THINK OF ROCKET RICHARD, you think of the Montreal Canadiens. When you think of Bobby Orr, you think of the Boston Bruins. When you think of Gordie Howe, you think of the Detroit Red Wings. Even though Gordie played for Houston and New England in the World Hockey Association and then Hartford, you will always think of Gordie wearing the red and white of the Red Wings. And why not? He played for a quarter of a century with them. But he did leave.

DON: Why did you leave Detroit?

GORDIE: I had to. I wanted to play with the youngsters, Mark and Marty, and there is another one—Murray—but he was a little too young. The reason I retired was because there was total confusion at the time in Detroit. The idea of hanging on [in Detroit] until they became of age to play the game, which was 20 [back then, players had to be 20 years old to be able to play in the NHL]—and [the WHA] found a loophole in the rules and picked up Marty and Mark and put them in the WHA, and then Bill Dineen came along and offered me my dream and I grabbed at it. It was a big thrill, and I have to thank Don Blackburn [the coach of the Hartford Whalers]. One game in Detroit, he started me, Mark and Marty. I'll always thank him for that. Hartford — Don, you didn't say nice things about that city. Then there was another factor that was called money.

DON: Every man has his price.

GORDIE: There was also the mushroom treatment.

DON: Tell us what that is.

GORDIE: Well, they keep you in the dark, and every once in a while feed you some manure.

Of course, Gordie was right about me knocking Hartford. When I coached the Bruins, we in the NHL thought of the WHA as a bunch of bush leaguers, and the people of Boston thought Hartford was not a real sports town. We felt it was beneath us to play an exhibition game against a WHA team, and especially against Hartford.

With Boston less than a two-hour car drive to Hartford, the Whaler fans thought of the Bruins as their rival. We barely knew the Whalers were a pro team. But money talks, and our GM, Harry Sinden, was offered a ton of dough to play an exhibition game against the Whalers.

It was the 1975 preseason, and back then exhibition games were not like today. Preseason games today are pretty tame and no one wants to get hurt. In the '70s they were tougher than the regular season. We had wars with the Philadelphia Flyers, Montreal Canadiens and just about everybody else. The Big Bad Bruins and the Broad Street Bullies, the Flyers, were the big draws in the NHL.

Every team wanted an exhibition game against us or the Flyers because they knew it was an instant sellout.

We had played about eight exhibition games in a short amount of time. Some of them were real wars; some had more than one bench-clearing brawl. Every game had a ton of fights, and with jobs on the line, the games got vicious. We were exhausted, but Harry couldn't resist the money and had us play the game in Hartford as we travelled back to Boston.

It was the last game of a grueling schedule of eight exhibition games, so we weren't thinking too much of the game. Then, when we walked into the building, there were signs all over the place: BEAT BOSTON, WELCOME TO REAL HOCKEY, WELCOME TO THE BIG TIME, BOSTON SUCKS, and so on. They were treating this game like the seventh game of the Stanley Cup. I was just shaking my head; it was just what we needed after playing eight hard-fought games. The Whalers players were sky high for the game. During the warm-up, the fans were giving it to us. The place was sold out and they wanted blood.

The players were not too happy. I told them, "Look, we have to play this game, like it or not. Let's be smart about it. The longer it goes and we don't score, the worse it will be. They'll start to build up some confidence. Let's blitz them right off the bat and run up a score. We'll get the crowd out of it and we can coast and take it easy later in the game."

The score was 6–0 at the end of the first. I just rested my vets for the rest of the game and played the third- and fourth-liners and young guys who didn't act like jerks. We were pretty quiet, just got the win and went home to the Boston Garden, two hours down the road.

To tell you the truth, it wasn't that we played so well, but their goalie had a rough night. I had a few things to say after the game. I said, "What kind of town is Hartford? They have a hockey team, but they don't have an airport," or something like that. The press made a big deal out of it, and there were editorials in the paper on how bad a guy I was. I was Hartford's Public Enemy Number One for a while. All those years later, Gordie still remembered that I knocked Hartford.

* * *

Gordie was like all of us back then: we just wanted to play hockey. Money and contracts were just a formality. Most of us had jobs in the summer and we didn't consider hockey "work"—it was fun and we would have played for free. Things slowly started to change, and in the late '60s and early '70s, hockey started to become more a "business" for the players. But Gordie was old school.

In 1968, hard rock defenceman Bobby Baun got traded to Detroit. Bobby, who had played 12 years in the NHL, sat down and had a chat with Gordie, who was in his 22nd NHL season. He gave Gordie a dose of reality.

> **DON:** How about when Baun went to Detroit? I don't know how it happened, but I was in the minors somewhere, I heard the story he sat down with you and asked how much money you were making.

> **GORDIE:** Well, I have to thank Bobby. Number one, he's such an honest individual and we've become very, very good friends. We went out for lunch one day he said, "Do you mind if I say something to you? You're stupid."

> **DON:** Just like that, he called you stupid.

> **GORDIE:** Yes. I said, "We all know that, but what is the reason?" Baun said, "Because I floated around in this league and I am making a lot more money than you are, and you're the laughingstock of the whole league." You have to understand

that when I went up to talk contract, before I got my wife, Colleen, which was the smartest move I ever made in the game of hockey, I'd say, "If I'm supposed to be the best player on the team, pay me accordingly." They said, "Don't worry about it." So at that time, I think there were three guys [on the team] making more money. Probably one of the reasons I was mad at Carl Brewer was because he making almost twice as much. It was my fault. I should have had a little more pride and stuck to it. But I just loved the game of hockey, and whatever they paid me I thought, "Great!"

DON: Did you have any animosity towards Jack Adams [the Red Wings' GM at that time]? Did you think he took advantage of you?

GORDIE: Jack Adams was a master of all hockey, as we all know. He was always on your back constantly, except when it came to bonuses. I went upstairs to see him because I was going to Florida and I needed some extra cash and said, "Jack, you said if I had a good year, I'd get a $1,500 bonus." Jack asked if he had said that, and I said yes. Jack called up and said, "Give the kid $1,500." He was that type of guy. But when it came down to the hard core, he was pretty tough. In fact, when I was a rookie and asked for that jacket for a signing bonus, he held it up for two years.

DON'T MESS WITH MR. ELBOWS

GORDIE PLAYED 26 SEASONS IN THE NHL and six in the WHA. He won four Stanley Cups, six Art Ross Trophies, six Hart Trophies and was 23 times an NHL All–Star. He scored over 800 NHL goals and had over 1,800 points. He was also an over a point-a-game player in the NHL playoffs.

And as we all know, Gordie was no shrinking violet. He had four seasons of over 100 minutes in penalties and a career 1,685 minutes in penalties. That's equal to about 28 full games in the penalty box. Even in today's tamer NHL, there is still an unofficial event that players call a "Gordie Howe hat trick." That is, of course, when you score a goal, get an assist and have a fight in the same game. Funny thing is, Gordie only did this once, in 1953 against the Leafs, when he scored a goal and got an assist and fought Fernie Flaman.

But here is the thing: I'm going to tell you a secret about Gordie getting a Gordie Howe hat trick that not many people know. In the first period of a game between the Leafs and Wings on October 11, 1953, Gordie first got an assist on Red Kelly's goal at around the 11-minute mark of the first period. Then Gordie scored to make it 2–0 Wings at 18:02 of the first period. Fernie must have been mad at Gordie, because the two fought 30 seconds later, at 18:33 of the first. So Gordie had an assist, goal and fight in less than half a period.

* * *

Now, we know there are a lot of good nicknames, and Gordie earned his: Mr. Elbows.

> **DON:** Now, you were known as one of the meanest guys in hockey. Is it true you'd give the elbows every chance you got?

> **GORDIE:** If I could [give 'em a shot], I would. To explain, sometimes I didn't know why I did some things. I did find out early in my career. The first game I played against the Toronto Maple Leafs, I went into the corner with Gus Mortson, he came up with an elbow and took three of my front teeth out. I decided if that was part of the game, I should be there first.

When you think about epic fights in hockey, most people think of Stan Jonathan vs. Pierre Bouchard or the Bob Probert and Tie Domi battles. One of the biggest battles Gordie had was with New York defenceman Lou Fontinato.

Lou was no pushover. He was six foot one and 195 pounds and was the first player in the NHL to have over 200 penalty minutes in one season. He played six years in the NHL and had over 1,200 minutes in penalties in total. His reputation grew when, in the 1958–59 season, *Look* magazine had a six-page pictorial of Lou flexing his muscles and shots of him in action on the ice.

You knew Gordie and Lou were going to tangle. Gordie and Lou had something going for a while. One of Lou's jobs when he played the Wings was to get in Gordie's face and try and throw him off his game.

DON: So tell us about you and Lou. You guys tangled even before the big fight.

GORDIE: That's one of the common errors players make. They don't study who's on the ice when you're playing against them. I happened to know Louie was out there [just before the big fight], but we went at it months before. During a game against the Rangers, I was leaning over with the idea if I could get a piece of Louie or the puck, [Alex] Delvecchio would have a shot on net. He saw me leaning over and he came back and rapped me on the nose. That blurs you up a little bit, and I started swinging and we both got a few minutes. I started dabbing here [Gordie started to touch his mouth] and he said, "What's a matter with your lip, Gordie?"

Have you ever been walking down the street and say, "I've been here before?" Well, I was skating down the ice [during the same game] and said, "I've been here before." He came back at me, I gave him this [Gordie makes a cross-checking gesture] and cut his ear. It was practically cut in half. He came back on the ice [later] with a turban on and I said, "What's the matter with your ear, Louie?" It was my turn.

So [a few weeks later,] there was a fight between Red Kelly and Eddie Shack behind the net. I'm leaning on the net, kind of enjoying this, and I thought, "He's out here." As I turned around, he had dropped his gloves at the blue line and was coming in. I pretended I didn't see him until I took the first swing and caught him right on the nose. Got him pretty good. Lou was tough. He needed surgery to fix it, but he finished the game. He's a great guy. Tough as they come.

The newspapers gave the same kind of account as Gordie did, but they went into a little more detail. The UPI article that went across the country had the headline RANGER'S NOSE BUSTED BY HOWE IN HOCKEY TILT. It went on to tell what happened:

> *Fontinato became enraged when he felt Howe was picking on New York rookie Eddie Shack. He challenged the Detroit star behind the Red Wings net and Howe accepted, whipping off his gloves and piling into "Leapin' Lou." Then, while officials and players stood by seemingly awed by the spectacle, Fontinato and Howe exchanged punches for almost a full minute before being pulled apart. "Howe's a pretty good fighter," Fontinato admitted later. "He kinda rearranged my nose. But I wasn't losing." . . . Fontinato wasn't the only player who spilled blood. Shack suffered a deep cut scalp when allegedly high-sticked by Howe seconds before the main event. Warren Godfrey of the Red Wings was hospitalized with a concussion, presumably received in a tussle with Shack, and Harry Howell of the Rangers had four stitches to his chin. Nobody knows who hit Howell.*

There were pictures of Lou in the hospital after he got his nose broken. Like Gordie said, there weren't too many guys as tough as Lou, but after this fight, the word was out not to mess with Mr. Elbows.

GORDIE HOWE THE HOCKEY DAD AND SHORT STICKS

WHAT WAS MR. HOCKEY LIKE AS A hockey dad? You have to wonder if Gordie gave any advice to Mark and Marty.

GORDIE: Advice comes easy. We all know that. But yes, I did, particularly if they asked for it. I was never . . . *we* were never— I should never say "I," Colleen was a great part of it. She drove them thousands of miles every winter to help them become what they are. One particular day, I forcefully took Marty into the garage and I locked the door and said, "You're going to shoot the puck my way, or else." Because he had the stupid flipping shot; he would flip the puck and his passes would come flipping over too, and they were very hard to handle.

DON: What advice would you give to hockey moms and dads?

GORDIE: I had a chance to talk to hockey families, and I basically told them you're blessed with two eyes and one mouth. So keep one shut and the other two open and let the kids enjoy the game.

For all you hockey parents, words to live by from Mr. Hockey.

* * *

I had to ask Gordie about his stick. He used a very short stick in his playing days.

DON: When I was in your training camp for a cup of coffee, the one thing I remembered was your short hockey stick. Why did you have such a short hockey stick?

GORDIE: Yes it was up to about here. [Check out the picture on page 118.] The main reason for that was that I had long arms and no shoulders. That's why I used my elbows, as you say. But I liked everything in front of me. I liked to change hands holding the stick, and a shorter stick made it easier.

DON: I heard somebody say it was so you could get the stick faster up into somebody's face. But we won't get into that.

Now, I know those of you who don't play hockey are wondering why I was asking about Gordie's stick. You're asking yourself, "Does it really make that much of a difference?" You bet it does. The wrong length of stick can hurt your career, or even help end it.

Gordie's short stick was good for him, but the kids today like a long stick, especially the smaller players. Players like the New York Rangers' Mats Zuccarello or Marty St. Louis. It makes them as tall as a six-footer.

I remember watching the Oilers' first-round pick in 2013, Darnell Nurse, when he was playing minor midget for the Don Mills Flyers. Darnell was great. When he wanted to be, he was one of the most dominating minor midget defencemen I've seen. The one thing I did notice was he had a short stick for his size. When he was playing minor midget at 16 years old, Darnell was already six foot three and 180 pounds. I told Tie Domi, whose son, Max, played with Darnell on the Flyers, to get Darnell to try to play with a longer stick. If he spread out with a longer stick, he could cut the rink in half. The first thing the Oilers did when they drafted him was to try and get him to use a longer stick.

It's tough on a kid to switch from a shorter stick to a longer one. With the shorter stick, you can handle the puck better, no doubt.

But a longer stick, especially with a smaller player, can help him get to a puck quicker. For the taller players, it makes them play more upright. The one danger with a shorter stick, especially for taller players, is that the shorter stick makes you hunch over and it makes you keep your head down.

To this day, I still feel the reason Eric Lindros got so many concussions was because, even though he was so big, he used a short stick and that cost him big time. When he played in the OHL for Oshawa, he was a monster. He was six foot four and close to 200 pounds. He could hit and score, and everybody was afraid of him and nobody wanted to take a run at him.

With the shorter stick, he felt he could handle the puck better and he got used to playing bent over a lot. Those are the key words—bent over a lot—meaning his head was down a lot. He was so big and he dominated in the OHL, so he didn't worry about getting hit, and that bad habit followed him to the NHL. There, players like Darius Kasparaitis, Hal Gill and the most dangerous of all, Scott Stevens, were waiting. As we know, Eric was never the same after Stevens nailed him. If you're a smaller player, it's good to have a longer stick, but for a bigger guy it makes sense to use a longer stick.

I know what you're thinking: "If Gordie had a shorter stick, how come he didn't get nailed like Eric did?" Are you kidding? You just read what happened to Lou Fontinato when he ran at Gordie.

WHAT GORDIE HOWE AND I HAVE IN COMMON

WHEN WE STARTED THE INTERVIEW, GORDIE and I were sitting on the set. I shook his hand, and I couldn't get over the size of his hands and what a strong handshake he had. Gordie was one of those guys who was strong but had sloped shoulders, and you could tell he was stronger than he looked. To me, he looked like a guy who worked on heavy construction all his life.

DON: I know that we have one thing in common. When you were young, you worked on construction. I see the guys now, and they lift 9,000 pounds of weights, but they can lose that awful fast. In construction, it builds you up differently. I heard you lifted cement bags.

GORDIE: I worked in the summer and I could lift four bags of cement that were about 80 pounds. It was good for your body with that kind of repetition.

I should explain what I mean when I say players can lose the muscles they get from lifting weights. If you lift weights to build muscle, and then you stop lifting the weights, you lose that muscle fast.

I'll give you an example. In Boston, we had a first-round draft choice, a great-skating defenceman, who could handle the puck, had a fair shot, but he was so skinny that if he stood sidewise, you couldn't see him. Well, in his second year, he decided to bulk up, and did he ever get big. When he came to training camp, he'd put on about 20 pounds of muscle. He was so looking forward to showing me how much stronger he had gotten over the summer.

But the first day of camp, he caught the flu bad. So bad that he tried to scrimmage and he ended up having to be helped off the ice. He couldn't keep anything down and just kept drinking liquids. He was laid up in bed for four days. When he came back, he was back to his skinny self. He seemed to have lost all the muscle he'd built up over the summer. I know you people are saying that's impossible, but I'm telling you the truth. That's what I mean when I say Gordie had construction-guy muscles, meaning that his muscles and strength weren't going away.

Believe me, it's not that we wanted to work in the summer. We had no choice. I'd come home from the season on a Friday and start working on the following Monday at the Kingston Public Utilities Commission. The jackhammer was my specialty. When you're on your feet 10 hours a day with a pick and shovel or a jack-hammer, it builds muscles that stay, no matter what. Gordie had those types of muscles; that's why he could still play good hockey when he was in his 50s.

I remember being at banquets with Gordie. He always walked very slowly when he entered a room. He was good at his speeches — he was no Red Storey or Dennis Hall, but who is? I always felt he was a little uncomfortable public speaking, but after the banquet is when Gordie shone. He was terrific when talking amongst the kids. Once, I was sitting at a table with Gordie and there was a lineup for autographs. A kid would shove a picture of Gordie at him for him to sign. He would just look at the kid then take his marker and touch the kid's hand gently. "What do you say?" Gordie would ask. If the kid didn't say "please" or "thank you" he would get the question from Gordie again. But then Gordie would always have fun with the kid. He was a real people's guy, that's why everybody loves Gordie Howe.

I finished this book during the 2016 playoffs. I was in San Jose when Ron and I heard the news that Gordie had passed away. All I can say is this: for all you players that play hockey in heaven, keep your head up, Gordie's coming.

CLIFF THORBURN

I asked Cliff, "What is the difference between snooker and pool?"

This is snooker . . .   . . . and this is pool.

THE SNOOKER PLAYER

ON AUGUST 28, 1985 OUR GUEST WAS WORLD snooker champion Cliff Thorburn from Victoria, British Columbia. Cliff was kind of a unique guest. In Canada, he wasn't that well known, but in England he was like Wayne Gretzky. Cliff won the world snooker championship in 1980 and was ranked Number 1 in the world. His big claim to fame in the snooker world was that he got a maximum break—that's sinking (in snooker they call it "potting") all 15 red balls with all 15 black balls, and then all six colour balls—in the 1983 world championship.

As I was getting ready for the show, Gerry Patterson came down to my dressing room, which was the room where the bar stored empty beer cases. I should have known something was up because Gerry never bugged me before a show.

I had a few suits hanging on a rack and Gerry asked me what suit I was going to wear for Cliff's show. I had picked out a rather tame-looking pinstripe, but Gerry suggested I wear one of my louder plaids.

I didn't think much of it and said, "Okay."

If you've never seen a snooker match, it's very posh—the players wear tuxedos and the whole nine yards.

So the show starts and I introduce Cliff, and he comes out in a beautiful tuxedo with a bow tie and a beautiful pair of shoes, shined to a mirror polish. Cliff was a tall, really good-looking guy and was dressed to the nines.

We sat down and started the show.

> **DON:** All the ladies in London say they like your sexy smile. Geez, you're so good-looking I don't know if I should shake your hand or kiss you. OK Cliff, for all of us that don't know, what is the difference between pool and snooker?

CLIFF: Really?

> **DON:** Yes. What's the difference?

Cliff ran his fingers down his tux.

CLIFF: Well, this is snooker . . .

And then he reached over and ran his fingers along my plaid jacket.

CLIFF: . . . and this is pool.

> **DON:** Kind of walked into that one, didn't I?

The crowd just roared. I didn't know what to say. Gerry had set the whole thing up and he got me good. It was one of the hardest the audience ever laughed at a show.

THE HUSTLER

WHEN I THINK OF POOL, I think of one of my favourite movies, the 1961 classic *The Hustler* starring Paul Newman as "Fast Eddie" Felson and Jackie Gleason as Minnesota Fats. Piper Laurie and George C. Scott were in it too. Paul Newman's best movie—after *Slap Shot*, of course. The movie was up for eight Oscars, including Best Picture, Best Actor and Best Supporting Actor. But I always wondered if it was a good "pool movie" in the eyes of a real pool (or snooker) player.

> **DON:** Now, did you start off as a hustler?

> **CLIFF:** I really don't resemble that remark. I started out playing in 1964 or '65 and I used to travel all across the country looking for all the good players, and I used to lose and lose and lose until I started to win. I'd go to Vancouver, to Montreal, and I was getting better as I was going along. Then I'd go back to the towns I hit months before and I was getting better all the time, so I had a pretty good run for four or five years. But I didn't really hustle, I just gambled, and after a year everybody knew who I was, so they were the ones trying to hustle me. I just wanted to play.

> **DON:** You saw the movie *The Hustler*. Now, were Jackie Gleason and Paul Newman any good, or were they a joke?

> **CLIFF:** I've never met either one of them, but I've heard a few stories. Apparently Jackie Gleason played for a living in New York for the longest time, just trying to make money and stay alive before he became a comedian and an actor. Paul Newman apparently had a lot of natural talent. Willie Mosconi, who was the technical advisor for the movie, said

they were naturals at the game and it didn't take them long to find their way around the table.

Cliff might not have been a hustler, but one of my best friends in hockey was. Brian "Killer" Kilrea and I met in 1959 when we played for the Springfield Indians and Eddie Shore. We've been good friends ever since, and most every year Brian and I coach the Canadian Hockey League Top Prospects Game together. Brian is the winningest coach in junior hockey history. Brian coached the Ottawa 67's for 29 years and had over 1,193 wins. But I know something most of the kids he coached didn't know. We had Brian on the show a couple of times and we talked about his time in the pool halls.

DON: Now, I know something nobody else knows. This guy, when he was 15, looked about 10, right? And you were a pool hustler. Tell us about that, a real pool hustler, you're looking at this guy right here.

BRIAN: I enjoyed pool and I learnt it well. When I was young, I graduated school early and I started taking pool serious, along with hockey. I came up to play junior hockey, and there was a couple of fellas that were on the team that were older than I was, and they'd played pool as well. After a couple of weeks and a couple of sessions, a player on my team came to me and he said, "You better not play pool anymore. Some of the guys are getting mad." I got older and I went to play pro hockey, and when I came back home in the summer, I never got a job—I played pool for a living, and my wife thought it would be nice if I went and got a job at a lesser pay so she could tell everyone what I worked [at] through the summer. And that's a true story. But I got to enjoy the game.

DON: Well, let's tell the story [about] when you were 15, when the guy used to pick you up and you used to go to the city. You didn't want to tell that one. Tell it!

BRIAN: Yeah, there was a fella, his name was Pauly, he started watching me play and he thought I was pretty good, so he'd come down and pick me up and he'd take me to different pool rooms around home. And because I looked young and looked easy, some of the fellas would come around and say, "Hey kid, you want to shoot a game for a couple of bucks?" or whatever. And in those days, we were talking back in the late '40s, and I'd say, "Yeah, I'll play." And so Pauly would tell me when I should try and when I should take it easy.

DON: Just like the movies!

BRIAN: And he drove me around, and he'd always bring me back so my parents didn't have to worry about me coming home late. And at the end of the day I couldn't be a loser, because if we won, he gave me something for playing; if we lost, he said, "Well, you learned." So I was fortunate . . . besides a hockey player, I got to know that side of the life, the gambling part, which has really helped me when I went on to hockey because you gamble in hockey as well as with coaching.

Brian and I were at a training camp in the late '60s and somehow we found ourselves at a bar with a bunch of NHLers. Goalie Gerry Cheevers, who I played with in Rochester, was shooting pool and cleaning up. Gerry was a great guy, but he really thought he was cool shooting pool that day. He was beating guys, taking their money.

I can still see him shooting pool with a cigarette hanging out of his mouth. I said, "Gerry, why don't you play Brian?"

Cheevers said, "Yeah, come on Brian, let's play."

Brian let Gerry win right up until they decided to play for some big dough, and then Brian just about ran the table.

Gerry didn't know, and hardly anybody knew, that Brian was a real-life "Fast Eddie" Felson.

Cliff said in the interview that the best players are the players who never get too high when they win or too low when they lose. You have to have nerves of steel when you are shooting one last ball at the end of the championship for all the marbles. Cliff was a great, soft spoken gentleman just like you'd expect a world class snooker player would be. I still have that plaid jacket and every time I see it in the closet I think of Cliff saying, "This is pool." And the more I look at it, the more I see he's right.

RED STOREY

My old buddy, author, NHL referee, Grey Cup hero, lacrosse great,
television and radio star and banquet speaker extraordinaire, Red Storey.

RED STOREY AND THE GREY CUP HAT TRICK

In 1993, we interviewed Red Storey. Most people know Red as
a longtime NHL referee. He had refereed over 480 regular-season
games, as well as seven consecutive Stanley Cup finals. A lot of
people didn't know that Red was also a great athlete. He played for
the Toronto Argonauts and won the Grey Cup in 1937 and 1938.

The same time he was playing football, he was also playing
lacrosse in the Ontario Lacrosse Association. He played senior
men's baseball and got an offer from the Philadelphia Athletics,
and he played hockey in New Jersey for the River Vale Skeeters.
You could almost say he was like Canada's Jim Thorpe.

Red was always giving me a hard time about wearing makeup
on TV, and he didn't pass up the chance to give me another shot.

RED: Before you start, what's all this malarkey wanting to put makeup on me for television with a face like I got? Because I always say,

> *"For beauty, I am no star*
> *There are others more handsome by far*
> *My face I don't mind it*
> *Because I sit behind it*
> *It's you people in front that I jar."*

DON: You know what I tell the makeup lady? It's tough to improve on perfection. Now, everyone knows you as a ref, but you played in the Grey Cup.

RED: Well, I was in two: 1937, we met Winnipeg and we beat them; in 1938, we met Winnipeg again. Starting the third quarter, they were leading, 7–6. It was a tough ball game. In the last 12 minutes, I got a little lucky.

DON: A little lucky? Get this: three TDs, one of them 102 yards, thank you very much.

Red seemed to brush off this achievement.

The newspapers at the time didn't. The *Winnipeg Free Press* (dated December 12, 1938) compared Red to the great Lionel Conacher.

> *In the vanguard of the swift point-producing assault on the western prestige was 20-year-old Red Storey, who gave a magnificent display of all-round effectiveness. He made the last quarter interminable for the Winnipeg adherents as he legged the ball up and down the field, producing touchdown after touchdown. . . . His individual unruffled display eclipsed anything in the way of heroics seen on the gridiron since the days of Lionel Conacher . . . he manufactured*

three touchdowns, one of them coming after a compelling 102-yard
dash for the shadows of his own goal post.

Didn't the press write great back then? It's almost poetic. Anytime
you're mentioned in the same sentence as Lionel Conacher,
Canada's greatest noted athlete, that's something.

After that great Grey Cup game in 1938, Red got offers to play
for the New York Giants and the Chicago Bears, but he said no.
His football days ended when he got a knee injury.

WATCH OUT FOR ROOKIES IN THE WARM-UP

I ASKED RED ABOUT HIS DAYS playing lacrosse. One of his stories
had a very familiar ring to it, and it reminded me of a low point
in my days of coaching the Rochester Americans in the AHL.
The lesson for all you coaches out there is you gotta watch out for
rookies in the warm-up.

> **DON:** Like I said, everybody thought you were just a ref. Tell us
> about you playing lacrosse.

> **RED:** It's funny, but I took up lacrosse on a dare. I played ball in
> Barrie in the Depression days, and they wouldn't pay me
> any money. But if you lived out of town, they would pay you
> to play ball. I was their best player and they wouldn't pay
> me. I said to them, "If you don't pay me, I'm going to Orillia
> and playing lacrosse." I never held a lacrosse stick in my life.
>
> Now, Orillia was the number one lacrosse team in the
> world, box lacrosse. They said, "Go ahead, you'll be home in
> a week." I went up to Orillia, I didn't know how to hold a
> stick, knew nothing about lacrosse, never played lacrosse in
> my life. Bucko McDonald was the playing coach and he
> gave me a tryout. I could run like hell, but I didn't know how

to play with the stick. The team used to practise an hour or an hour and half, then go shower and take off. I go around and sneak back into the building, and I worked out three or four hours a day by myself, throwing the ball against the wall and learning how to catch it and all that.

Now a month of training has gone by and it's opening game, and I walk into the dressing room and my sweater is hanging on the wall. I can't believe I'm dressing—the best team in the world, and I made it playing for a month. I'm so happy, you got no idea. Now, at the start of the game, they turn out all the lights in the building and they turn on the spotlights. The stands were loaded, and most of the fans were, too. They announce your name and you come running onto the floor. I'm so happy I don't have to go back to Barrie and play ball that I'm two feet off that floor running out there. Now they got both teams introduced and they turn on all the lights, and it's opening night, the first game I've ever played in my life.

Tradition says the youngest rookie has to take the first warm-up shot on the goalie. I'm the youngest rookie, so they hand me the ball. So they throw me the ball, I go back to the centre of the floor—like I said, I could run like hell. So I come running in there as hard as I could, I wind up and I take a shot, and I broke our goalkeeper's jaw.

DON: And they kept ya?

RED: Yep, they kept me. I thought I was going back to Barrie, but they kept me.

Let me explain why—or, I should say, how—Red broke the goalie's jaw. Red didn't know how to warm up the right way. The goalie was not expecting a shot at his head. He was relaxed, expecting a warm-up shot like the other players would shoot.

Red was all fired up and wanted to impress the coach or someone, so he really fired it and caught the goalie unawares. The result was a broken jaw. I'm sure the coach was not impressed.

When Red said he broke the goalie's jaw, the audience laughed. I guess it was a funny story, but I didn't laugh. I knew how the coach of Orillia must have felt, because it happened to me, and let me tell you, folks, it's not funny.

It was 1971, and I had been made the coach of the Rochester Americans. I couldn't get a job that summer before, not even sweeping floors, so I got on my knees and asked the Lord, "What am I going to do?"

I swear to you, a voice said to me, plain as day, "Go back and play hockey."

I started to get in shape, met the coach and GM of Rochester, Doug Adam, and asked for a tryout. He agreed. It was a long shot, but I made the team. To make a long story short, I wasn't playing or even dressing much, even though I was playing well.

The team wasn't playing that well, and the Rochester fans were not too happy. One game, the team got hammered pretty good and a fan came down and sucker punched Doug Adam to show his displeasure.

The next day, Adam made me coach. I heard him say, "Coaches are hired to be fired." To him, I was a sacrificial lamb. He had to pay me anyway, so why not make me the coach? He didn't have to pay me more money, and no way the team was going to make the playoffs. He figured when we missed the playoffs, that would be the excuse to fire me after the season was over.

I figured if we made the playoffs, he couldn't fire me. I had no job or trade to go back to, so it was make the playoffs or I didn't know how I was going to feed my family. We were about 10 points out of a playoff spot with about half the season to go. I figured I had to win about half the games to make the playoffs. We went on a pretty good run and won 16 of the last 38 games, with five ties, and we needed one more win to clinch a playoff spot.

The final game was in Springfield against the Kings. We were one point behind the Providence Reds. We win, we're in; we lose, we're out.

Now, the Vancouver Canucks owned Rochester. Doug Adam came down in the dressing room before the game and wanted me to play a goalie named Serge Aubry. He got the word from Vancouver that they wanted Aubry to start. Not sure why, but that was what I was told to do.

Serge hadn't played a lot of games down the stretch, and I was planning to play Lynn Zimmerman. Lynn had played most of the games for me and had a strong goals-against average of 3.50, pretty good back in those days. Serge was struggling a little and his average was close to 5.00 in the games he played.

I told Doug there was no way I was going to put Serge in. He was furious, and I knew for sure my fate was sealed if I didn't win. He then told me that Vancouver also wanted me to play a rookie who hadn't played much at all that season. I wasn't even going to dress the kid, but I thought, "I'll dress him and just not play him."

I was in the dressing room during the warm-up, pacing up and down like most coaches do. I looked up, and the trainer, in a state of shock, said, "Grapes, bad news. Zimmy's hand is broken."

I knew right away what happened. "I know who broke his hand. It was the rookie. Right?"

He just shook his head yes.

The same situation as Red breaking his goalie's jaw. Zimmy was relaxed, never expecting a shot at his head. The rookie let one fly too high, so by instinct, Zimmy brought up his hand to protect himself and it hit the underside of the blocker glove and broke his hand.

Even though we outshot them badly, we lost the game by one goal and missed the playoffs by one point to Providence.

At the end of the season, Doug called me into his office and said, "Don, you did a great job, but we're making a change in your department."

I thought to myself, "Now, who is in my department? Well, there's me, and . . . me!"

So I was fired. But then Rochester was sold to some business- men that summer, and I was made coach and GM. The Lord works in mysterious ways.

So during the interview with Red, I could just imagine how the Orillia coach felt, because I had had that same feeling. Total dis- aster as your season swirls down the drain.

* * *

Red mentioned Bucko McDonald. Most people have not heard of Bucko, but you could say he changed the game of hockey.

Wilfred Kennedy "Bucko" McDonald was born in 1911 in Fergus, Ontario. Bucko ended up playing for over 12 seasons in the NHL and won three Stanley Cups—two with the Red Wings, in 1936 and '37, and one in 1942 with the Leafs.

Bucko was also a great lacrosse player. He won the Mann Cup with the Brampton Excelsiors, but hockey was his game. He was a tough, hard-nosed defenceman. He was five foot ten and over 200 pounds. He was a fierce competitor, and Leafs owner Conn Smythe loved him.

Conn ended up buying him from the Wings early in the 1938–39 season for $10,000, a lot of money back in those days. After he won the Cup with the Leafs, he went to the New York Rangers.

After leaving the NHL, Bucko became the member of Parliament for Parry Sound, Ontario, from 1945 to 1949, and for Parry Sound–Muskoka from 1949 to 1957. In 1958, he went on to coach the Rochester Americans.

I always thought that Bucko McDonald switched Bobby Orr from forward to defence. But in Bobby's interview he said that it was Royce Tennant. I wonder what coach Tennant saw in Bobby that made him think he should be a defenceman? Bobby said he could read the play coming and going better from the defence's point of view. I'll bet Royce saw Bobby's talent and wanted him on the ice more. What a super move and now Royce gets the credit he deserves.

RED STOREY'S LAST GAME

IN SPORTS, A LOT OF REFS retire with a nice, quiet acknowledgement from the league and then go discreetly into retirement. Not Red. He went out with a bang.

DON: Now, let's get to it. You reffed 9,000 games and all, but you remember April 4, 1959—

RED: It was in Chicago, and I'm lucky I'm here.

DON: Tell us about that game.

RED: Ya gotta remember, Chicago was in the bottom of the league for years and Montreal was at the top of the league for years. All of a sudden, Chicago got Ted Lindsay from Detroit, Glenn Hall from Detroit, and [Eddie] Litzenberger from Montreal and a few more. They got six players in Chicago to build up the team. So now they're in the semifinals, and it's the sixth game against Montreal and the winner goes to the Stanley Cup finals. They got 20,000 people in the building. They used to say 16,000 but there were 20,000.

It was a great game. Fabulous. You couldn't hear. All three officials had to blow the whistle to stop the play. And what happens was this. It was a very close game. Eddie Litzenberger was a big guy like me and was one of their leading scorers. He comes waltzing out of his own end and Marcel Bonin from Montreal puts his stick flat on the ice, trying to knock the puck off of Litzenberger's stick.

Litzenberger, who was awkward as I am, steps on the stick. He goes flying up in the air. All the Chicago team, well, they quit skating and are waiting for me to call a penalty. There is no penalty. He stepped on the guy's stick—I can't give him a penalty. Before they get their sense back, Montreal scores a goal. Now there is a little bit of a disturbance.

DON: Slightly.

RED: Yes, just slightly. Now they can see their chances of going to the finals slipping. This was late in the third period. It took us about 20 minutes to get the game started.

DON: Tell us about Doug Harvey.

RED: First of all, this was only one episode that night. I'm ready to drop the puck at centre ice and someone yells, "Look out, Red!" I turn around and this guy is running on the ice towards me with a pail of beer and he throws it right in my face. I grab him, and Doug Harvey grabs him on the other side. Doug knew me and my temper. He could see I'm getting ready to hit him and Doug says, "Red, you can't hit a fan." Doug goes *bang* and he hits the guy.

He knows I'm still going to hit him. Doug says, "Red, don't hit a fan, you can't hit a fan," and *bang*, he hits him again. The guy staggers off the ice, and now Doug was the only guy on the ice with me. Everyone else was hiding in the nets or along the boards. The fans were throwing chairs, bottles, everything.

I stood at centre ice. I figured any guy that's going to hit me, he has to have a pretty good arm. Doug stayed with me. All of a sudden, Doug yells, "Look out, Red!" A guy climbed over the screen—they had screen in those days [instead of glass]. He was about to jump on my back, and I saw his shadow and I duck and flip him over my back into the air. While the guy was in the air, Doug cut him [with his stick] for 18 stitches.

DON: Can you imagine if you did that now? I bet a guy didn't come on the ice again after that.

RED: Nobody came on the ice after that. The game is over and a player on Chicago named Danny Lewicki—a good friend of mine; they were all good friends of mine. Believe it or not, the only friends a referee has in the world are the guys he is controlling on the ice. If you're fair with them, they'll be on your side. Anyway, the game is over and Danny Lewicki comes over to me and says, "Red, here's my stick. You're gonna need it now more than I do."

In the old Chicago building, you go out the end of the rink and down those stairs. There was a row of seats right there, and there were six hoodlums sitting right there. I got news for you, I opened up the whole six of them with the stick. I cleaned house. I don't go down those stairs if I don't clean them out first.

DON: Boy, hockey was great back in those days. But that was your last game.

RED: True story. That was my last game in the National Hockey League. That was one of the best games I reffed in the NHL. But we had a president [Clarence Campbell], and he was the supervisor of that series. With two and a half minutes to go in the game, I don't know if I should call the game off because of the riot or what to do. I sent for him, and he refused to come down to the bench to make a decision or help me make a decision. He said he feared for his safety. And *I* was the one they wanted to kill.

My next game was in Boston. It was Boston and Toronto. I'm in Boston, and Eddie Powers is my standby official. George Hays and Bill Morrison are my linesmen. Now, we're over at Sharky's bar, having a few Cokes.

DON: You mean a few pops?

RED: Pops? Okay, let's not kid ourselves, we were having a few brews. A kid comes running through with the papers. I said, "Give me one of each." I heard rumours that there were things being said about me.

What happened next was the last straw for Red. NHL president Clarence Campbell went to the papers and blasted Red. He blamed him for the riot that went on in Chicago.

DON: So what did they say in the papers?

RED: Well, we're having a few pops, as you say. I read the headlines. "STOREY CHOKES"—CAMPBELL. What the hell is this? "STOREY FROZE"—CAMPBELL. I looked at Eddie and said, "Eddie, you better go back and get a night's rest. You're refereeing tomorrow night." He said, "No, *you're* refereeing." I told him, "I'll never ref again in that league. I cannot accept that and work in the National Hockey League and face my family. Go and get a night's rest."

I walked the streets of Boston all night because I didn't know what to do. I had a wife and two kids to keep. I was really worried about it. The next day, I called a press conference and I gave them the story I was quitting. That spring, one of the governors of the league came to Montreal for the board of governors meeting, and he came to me and asked me how much money would it take to get me back to the National Hockey League. I told him it wouldn't take any money at all because money is not my object. He asked me what I wanted. I wanted a public apology in every paper in the world that Mr. Campbell was quoted.

He said, "That's all you want? No problem, Red. I'll phone you after the meetings and let you know how it went." He phones me after the meetings and says, "Red, I'm afraid I got bad news for you. Mr. Campbell will not apologize. He will not retract the statement. He stood there at the meeting and said, 'Don't worry about Red, fellas. Red is so stupid, he doesn't know how to feed his family. He'll be back here on his hands and knees in September, begging for his job back.'"

I said, "You go back and tell Mr. Campbell to hold his breath till I ask for my job back." That's the whole story right there.

Eddie Powers went on to ref that game between Boston and Toronto. The first period didn't go too well for Eddie. The game was getting pretty rough and he called 11 penalties that period.

The Boston crowd didn't like that at all, and over 13,000 Boston fans started to chant, "We want Storey."

Eddie only called one more penalty for the rest of the game.

That whole year, things were not very good between the refs and the NHL. Many refs felt the NHL didn't have their backs. In a press article that ran in 1959, Eddie Powers made that clear.

"I'm 100% behind Red. . . . The front office has not backed up the officials this year. We don't work under an ideal situation. Let the record this year talk for itself. There has been criticism of our work and nothing has been done about it."

As the story started to grow, Mr. Campbell said that the comments about Red were told in confidence to an Ottawa reporter and were never meant to be made public. But the backlash grew against the

NHL, and it seemed everyone supported Red.

The *Montreal Star*'s Elmer Ferguson wrote, "When the league president, who should back, not criticize, his officials, makes such public declarations as are credited to him, Storey manfully walked out. . . . He couldn't, in fact, do anything else and retain his self-respect."

Baz O'Meara, also of the *Montreal Star*, wrote, "Storey did the only thing that a man with gumption could do . . . he emerges from this mess with considerable stature."

Even though Red walked away from a $10,000-a-year job—good money in those days—he came out of the whole thing smelling like a rose.

DICK BEDDOES, SANTA, HAROLD BALLARD AND A FAKE ROSE

ONE OF RED'S FAVOURITE STORIES, AND what quickly became a broadcasting classic, was the day Red dressed up as Santa for a midweek game.

DON: Tell us about the time you met Harold on TV.

RED: Well, I was doing some TV at the time, and after the game, they would have people talking about the game and such. One day around Christmas, Dick Beddoes and Harold Ballard were on after the game. Ralph Mellanby [the producer] asked me to dress up like Santa and go on air and do a little bit. So I get dressed up and head on set and say, "Ho ho ho, Merry Christmas!" Ballard looks up at me and says, "Hello Santa, you old fart." I didn't know what to say. Beddoes tried to help me out and says, "Well, Santa, what did you get Harold for Christmas?" I looked at Harold. "Well, Dick, there's only one thing to get a man who has everything. Penicillin!"

Dick Beddoes and Harold were quite a pair on television, and you never knew what was coming. I fell victim to them on one of my first television appearances.

Of course, Harold was owner of the Toronto Maple Leafs and was a colourful character. Dick was a sportscaster on CHCH-TV in Hamilton, Ontario. He wore a hat and dressed in a way he thought was spiffy.

He was terrific on TV. Sharp as a razor blade, and he showed no mercy when you went on air with him. You'd better be ready when you went on with those two.

I wasn't. I was a rookie, I had only been on the air for a month, and I was told by Ralph Mellanby to go on after the game with those two wolves.

I went on set and said hello to Dick and Harold. They seemed friendly enough as they started to count us down to going live on air. Three, two, one, and we're live.

Dick looks at the rose I was wearing and said, "That's a fake rose you're wearing. What else is fake on you?"

Harold roared with laughter. I was speechless. Dick showed no mercy on me. To say the least, it was embarrassing. I hadn't been on TV all that much and I didn't know how to handle it. But as they say, revenge is a dish best served cold.

Jump ahead two years. Now I had been on TV and radio a lot, and I knew the score. You couldn't catch me on anything, and I could hold my own with Dick or anybody else.

I was helping Dick on a live radio show called *Jock Talk*, and I was ready to get back at Dick for what he did to me when I was a rookie.

We were taking questions from fans calling in to the show.

One caller asked me, "Grapes, what do you do with your old clothes?"

I said, "Well, when I'm done with them, I give them to Dick."

Dick kind of got mad and started saying that he was a better dresser than me. I kept giving him shots about his clothes and hats, and he started to get a little madder. The callers started to chime in that I was a better dresser than Dick. The madder Dick got, the more I made fun of him.

It was great fun. Imagine, he really thought he was as good a dresser as me!

They are both gone now and I sure do miss them.

RED, ME AND THE RUBBER CHICKEN CIRCUIT

RED WAS A GREAT REFEREE. I know the word *great* gets thrown around a lot these days, but believe me, he was great. He had a great feel for the game. He did what few refs do today—he could control the game. The players loved him, as you can see by Red's story of Doug Harvey and Danny Lewicki during the riot in Chicago.

He refereed in the AHL when I played in the minors. He'd talk to the players, and the players loved that. If you were acting up, he would come up behind you and say, "Smarten up, Number 2, or next time you'll get a penalty."

That's why the players loved him. He talked to them and treated them fair and square. They respected him and wouldn't show him up or make him look bad.

I remember one of our players, in a fit of anger, threw his stick in the air. Red said, "If that stick comes down you're getting a misconduct."

People loved to hear Red tell his tales. In the 1980s, I was on the rubber chicken circuit, doing a dog and pony act with Red all across Canada. I did a lot of banquets back then and saw a lot of different speakers. Red was the best.

There were only two guys you never, ever followed if you had to give a speech at a banquet. One was Dennis Hull and the other was Red. The crowds just loved Red and he would end up having them eating out of his hand. They couldn't get enough of him, and that's why you never followed Red. If you did, you were bound to fail.

I will always remember, Red and I were in some small town out west doing our dog and pony act. We had done a few banquets in a row in different small cities and we were a little punchy. Both of us were getting ready to leave the hotel for the banquet, after which we'd head off to the next small town to do it all over again.

I dropped by his room on the way to the car, and I found Red in a real tizzy. He had just lost his wallet, with all his money, credit cards, driver's licence and such. He was in a real panic. His face was red and he was sweating buckets. He had torn his room apart looking for his wallet.

Just to bug Red, I asked, "Well, where did you put it, Red?"

Rose always did that to me, and I'd get mad. It got Red mad as well. "If I knew where I put it, it wouldn't be lost!" he bellowed. He said he thought he had put it on the cabinet by the bed.

I looked around, and sure enough, there was that wallet, stuck between the wall and the cabinet. I thought Red was going to give me a kiss, he was so happy and relieved. We went to the banquet and he knocked them dead as usual.

We had Red on the *Grapevine* a few times, and he was an audience favourite. With Red as the guest, it was like a night off for me. He was one of the easiest interviews I ever did. All I'd say is, "Red, remember the time when . . ." and he'd go off on a story.

I'd do that three times and the interview was over, and as usual, the audience was rolling on the floor.

Red was the very best. God love him.

BOB PROBERT AND DINO CICCARELLI

Here is the Dino the Dinosaur toy that broke right
after this taping. Dino was not too happy.

PROBERT AND DINO THE DINOSAUR

BOBBY ORR DREW THE BIGGEST CROWD we ever had, but a close
second was when we had Bob Probert and Dino Ciccarelli.

The show was taped in August 1993. Dino had scored his 450th
career goal and was coming off one of his biggest years, with 41 goals
and 97 points. Probert was the reigning heavyweight champion of
the NHL and maybe the most popular guy in Detroit. Everywhere
you went, everybody had a Probert sweater. It was electric.

Bob was kind of a shy, quiet person. It's funny that almost all
the tough guys are like that—kind of shy and very soft-spoken. As
we were getting ready for the show, standing off camera, I came
over to say hello.

I have to tell you, he kind of looked like the lead singer of the

Doors, Jim Morrison. Only a lot bigger. Bob's hair was standing on end and looked a little wild.

I said to him, "Bob, what's with the hair?"

He said, "Sorry, Grapes. I'm having a bad hair day."

The show started, and when I introduced Bob, the place went nuts. I always wondered why Bob never wore tie-downs. Now, for you folks who don't know what tie-downs are, they used to just be for the fighters, but now all players have a little strap that is sewn on the inside of their sweaters, near the bottom, and then the strap is attached to the player's pants. So if they get into a fight, the other guy can pull the sweater over their heads.

DON: Here he is, Bob Probert. Now, what would I do without you? The star of *Rock'em Sock'em* 5 and 4. Well, the star of *all* the *Rock'em Sock'em.* I'm going to ask you a question; I was a pretty good fighter in my day. I don't know if I would have been able to take this guy. I don't know if this happens to you, but after a fight, I'd always have a stiff neck from the guys pulling on the sweater.

BOB: Yep, that happens.

DON: Willi Plett [a real tough guy who played in the late '70s and early '80s] took his sweater and cut it down the back and then sewed it up. When the [other] guy pulled on the sweater, it would just tear and save his neck. But you don't even tie yours down.

BOB: Well, I used to, but then for a while I tried it the other way and it seemed to work. I just forgot one day . . .

Then someone from the audience yelled, "He doesn't need tie-downs!" He was right.

Now, in Detroit from 1985 to 1990, there were the Bruise Brothers, Bob Probert and Joey Kocur. The Red Wings drafted both Bob and Joey in 1983. A few years later, they were the most popular Wings. In the stands, you saw more Probert number 24 sweaters than any other sweater. Bob was the NHL heavyweight champ, but Joey was maybe the hardest puncher ever in the NHL.

If you ever happen to meet an NHL enforcer, take a look at his hands.

DON: Now, Joey Kocur—you two are the Bruise Brothers—now his hands are really bad. How come you don't hurt your hands?

BOB: Well, I've been lucky. Joey had a bad experience his first year in the minors. He hit someone in the tooth and it got infected and he almost lost his arm. They had to operate on it, and he has a big scar on his arm now.

DON: Ya know, a lot of guys, when they fight, just want to hit the guy. Joey wants to put it out the back of your head. Now, Gretzky admitted that Marty McSorley [his LA teammate and enforcer] is the most popular guy in LA. Now, it's not for all the pretty goals Marty scores. Now, I'm going to mention the guy in Winnipeg—now, take it easy—Tie Domi is the most popular guy in Winnipeg, and when I got to Detroit, all I see is number 24 in the stands. We all know why.

Today, a lot of people remember Bob for his epic battles with Tie, Troy Crowder and Wendel Clark and only think of him as a fighter. In the 1987–88 season, Bob had almost 400 minutes in penalties, which included 23 fights. But that year, Bob finished third in team scoring with 29 goals and 67 points. That year in the playoffs, Bob played 16 games and scored 21 points.

* * *

I was getting changed to do the second show with Dino Ciccarelli. Dino's rookie season in Minnesota, the fans gave him the nickname Dino the Dinosaur.

He had a good rookie season, scoring 18 goals in 32 games. In the playoffs, Dino took off. He scored 14 goals and 21 points in 19 games. During this run, Dino got the nickname.

Dino helped the North Stars go all the way to the finals, but they lost to the Islanders. The Minnesota North Stars started to give out blow-up Dino the Dinosaur toys at the game. They looked like Fred Flintstone's pet named Dino. Dino's mom and dad came to the show and brought one of these 13-year-old Dino the Dinosaur blow-up toys.

Between shows, the cameraman was getting shots of the toy. When he was done, he left it on the stage. Bob was waiting for the next show to start, and he picked up the toy to have a closer look. He just touched it, and the thing went *pop* and then deflated.

The whole audience went silent. You could see Bob didn't mean to do it, but Dino got really mad. He started in on Bob.

Bob was apologetic and said, "Dino, why would I want to break your dinosaur?"

Dino kept giving it to Bob until you could see Bob starting to get a little mad. Then Dino said, "I know you didn't mean it."

Things calmed down, but when I came on set I didn't know what was going on, but I could feel that something had happened. I saw the broken toy and said, "Hey Dino, what happened to your dinosaur?" Tim told me what happened and how funny it was to see this little banty rooster Dino Ciccarelli, all five foot ten of him, giving heck to six-foot-three Bob Probert.

PROBERT AND ALL THE YOUNG GUNFIGHTERS

DON: I'm gonna tell you a true story. I was in New Jersey and Troy Crowder was there—now, this was two years before he had his fight with you—so I'm sitting in the stands after the morning skate, and he came up to me and said, "Yo, Grapes. I'm as tough as Probert." I said, "Sure you are, kid." He said, "Someday I'll prove it." That's the way it is: two years before they had a good go, he was talking about playing Bob. Do you find it tough—every city you go in, there's a young gunfighter, and if he ever beats Probert, it's a feather in his cap. You must find it tough.

BOB: It's happened a lot in the past, but ya know, at times it gets old. But it's a job for me, and I have to stand up for my reputation I guess.

Bob and Troy Crowder did meet. On October 4, 1990, the Wings were playing in New Jersey. It was about halfway through the second period and they both dropped their gloves.

It was a pretty even fight until—and like we said earlier, Bob didn't have his sweater tied down—Troy got Bob's sweater over his head and got a couple of shots in.

Bob was cut over the right eye. Everyone in hockey was talking about the fight and the rematch that was coming. Remember, back then there was no way to see this game if you didn't live in the Detroit area.

It was only a matter of time before Bob and Troy were going to have a rematch of the New Jersey fight. They met again 50 games later, on January 28, 1991.

So Ron MacLean and I decided to drive to Detroit and see the rematch. *Hockey Night in Canada* phoned to get us tickets, but they told them, "Are you kidding? We've been sold out for months and there is no room in the press box."

I wouldn't have sat in the press box anyway. But they finally came through and got Ron and me tickets way up in the nosebleed section.

As we were walking into the arena, we saw the two linesmen for the game, Brad Lazarowich and Jerry Pateman. I walked over to them and said (not jokingly), "If they want to go, don't step in and break them up."

One of them said, "Are you kidding? We want to see this one too."

As we made our way to our seats, there was a buzz in the crowd, just like before a championship fight. The game started, but nobody paid attention to the play.

About halfway through the game, Bob and Troy got on the ice together. The puck went to the other end of the ice, but all eyes were on the two stars of the night. Both dropped their gloves at the same time, and it was a beauty.

Bob still didn't have his tie-downs on, and Troy was trying to get his sweater off like he did in the first fight. Bob hit Troy so hard his helmet went 10 feet in the air.

I have to say the fight was worth the drive. They both gave the fans their money's worth. You couldn't hear yourself think, it was so loud. They battled again in the third. Troy was right—he was a good fighter and he more than held his own.

For my money, Probert won the return match by a hard-earned decision. It lived up to its billing and all the fans went home happy, talking about the fight.

Now, let me tell you what happened after the fight. Ron and I decided that we had a four-hour drive back to Toronto, so we would leave early. There were a lot of Canadians in the crowd, and Detroit gets "Coach's Corner," so as we got up to leave, the crowd started to cheer. It was just a few at first, but then it grew to the section we were sitting in, and then the next section, so it was quite a commotion.

There was a faceoff in New Jersey's end, and one of the linesmen and the two centres were getting ready to drop the puck. They saw the ovation we were getting, and the centre backed off and looked up at the crowd. I swear the one linesman waved as if to say, "See? We didn't step in and break them up."

Fans were running up and shaking our hands and taking pictures and we couldn't move. The police came and escorted Ron and me through the crowd and got us to an elevator.

The police pushed Ron off the elevator and said, "No fans allowed!"

I said, "That's OK, officer, let him on."

It was the end of a perfect night.

DINO AND STANDING IN FRONT OF THE NET

We interviewed Dino and Bobby in 1993, and that year they had lost to the Leafs in the first round of the playoffs. It was a great series. The Leafs won in seven games, with Game 7 going into overtime. Nik Borschevsky tipped in a shot from Bob Rouse to give Pat Burns and the Leafs the win.

During the interview, we showed a highlight of Dino standing in front the net, getting hacked by Leafs goalie Félix Potvin. I mean, Dino was standing in front and getting worked over by Leafs defencemen Jamie Macoun and Sylvain Lefebvre, and then Potvin took his stick and chopped Dino's legs like a lumberjack chopping down a tree. Then, after the whistle blew, Potvin hammered Dino with his blocker on the back of the head twice. Probert came storming in and clocked Potvin, and then everybody got into it.

> **DON:** It's nice to have Number 24 [Bob Probert's number] around when things are going tough, isn't it?

> **DINO:** Yeah, it really is. Bobby, he's a heck of a player, and Bobby and I, we had the same roles on our power play. You know, we had the best power play in the league this year, and we have two units that go out. And Bobby and I have the same

roles on the power play, and unfortunately, I wish I had some of Probe's size.

DON: You and Potvin had things going, you know, that was unbelievable last year.

DINO: Well, we've got so many gifted players that can pass around the perimeters. We need guys like myself and Probe, somebody's got to get in front of him because the puck eventually has gotta get there and Potvin didn't like me standing there, but it wasn't gonna change my game.

DON: Funny, he never ever whacked around Bobby. Isn't that funny?

Around seven years after this interview, both Dino and I were owners of OHL teams. I owned the Mississauga Ice Dogs and Dino owned the Sarnia Sting.

I went up to Sarnia to look at a player that we were thinking of getting in a trade. Sarnia was playing their archrivals, the London Knights, who were owned by Dale and Mark Hunter.

There was a lot of hate between these two teams, from the players right up to the owners. Dino asked me to sit in his private box so we could get away from the crowd.

London jumped out to a 3–0 lead about five minutes into the game. Dino was just seething. The ref called a penalty on London, and Sarnia went on the power play. The Sting got four or five good shots, but nobody was standing in front of London's goalie and he had no problem. It was like picking cherries.

I could see Dino was not too happy. Then Sarnia got another power play, and the same thing: nobody in front of the net. Lots of shots and no goals.

A third penalty, and the same thing. Dino turned to me in a controlled rage. His face was scarlet red (now, I'm going to clean this up, but you can imagine some of the more colourful language I cut out) and he said, "You know, Grapes, I scored over 600 friggin' goals in the NHL. A lot of them standing in front of the friggin' net on the power play—that's where I made my living. You'd think I could get someone from the team I own to stand in front of the friggin' net. But I can't go down and say anything, because now it would be 'Dino the interfering owner.' What the friggin' type of power play has no one standing in front of the friggin' net?"

One more power play, no one standing in front of the net. Dino got up and looked at me, and then shook his head and walked out the door.

We never did make that trade.

Dino and Bob were my kind of guys; asked no quarter and gave none. Dino had a lot of injuries but never backed down from anybody. He was never drafted because of a broken leg when he was young. But he kept going and went on to set records. If Dino was playing in the NHL today he'd be making about $8 million a year.

Bob was the toughest guy in the league, a policeman that scored 29 goals. He was one of the shyest, quietest gentlemen you'd ever meet. He left us way too young. God Bless Him.

KEN DRYDEN

Ken talking about a save he made when
he was playing in the AHL.

THE FIRST TIME I SAW KEN DRYDEN,
AND THE SAVE THAT CHANGED MY LIFE

THE FIRST TIME I SAW KEN Dryden play, I was at one of the
lowest points in my life. It was in the 1970–71 season and I had
just retired and gone to work full time on construction. Late that
summer, I was laid off and I couldn't find a job.

Unfortunately, I had a lot of time on my hands and I went to
see the Rochester Americans and the Montreal Voyageurs play
at the War Memorial. Ken had played college hockey at Cornell
University and was an unknown and a bit of an oddity. Most goalies
were not that big back in those days, and Ken was six foot four, so
on skates he was close to six foot seven.

That game, he stood on his head. He had over 60 shots on him
and the score ended up a 2–2 tie. One of the greatest goaltending
performances I ever saw. Little did I know that, a few years later,

I would be behind the Bruins bench, trying to beat Ken and the Canadiens.

That same year, he went up to play six games for the Canadiens, and his record was 6–0 with a 1.65 goals-against average and a save percentage of .957. As usual, Boston and Montreal were going to meet in the first round of the playoffs. The Bruins were heavily favoured—they were defending Stanley Cup champions, having won the season series five games to one, scoring almost 400 goals that season and finishing 24 points ahead of Montreal.

It went seven games but Montreal beat the Bruins and went on to win the Cup. Ken won the Conn Smythe Trophy, and then the next year won rookie of the year in the NHL.

We interviewed Ken in 1983. He was very quiet and thought about his answers.

> **DON:** Ya know, Ken, you're retired now and I wish you would have retired years earlier and I might have had some Stanley Cup rings. [Funny thing is, Ken shook his head no. Did he mean I wouldn't have won some Stanley Cups, or that he wasn't going to retire early?] Now, do you remember that game in Rochester?

> **KEN:** I do, and the one thing I remember was I had a shutout for about 55 minutes, and Duke Harris scored the first goal, and then someone scored with a minute or so to go. If you remember, earlier in that game, somebody for Rochester came in and took a shot, and it went right into my glove and I didn't know where it was. The Rochester player didn't know where it was. The goal judge didn't know where it was. The referee didn't know where it was. Because no one knew where the puck was, the Rochester player put his stick up in the air and started celebrating, then the whole Rochester team started celebrating. The goal judge saw all

the players celebrating and must have thought that the goal went in, so he switched on the goal light. I look down at my glove, and the puck is in the goal glove. I'm going, maybe there were two pucks in this game and I had one of them right here. I skate out to argue with the referee, and all my teammates are pushing me away, saying, "No, no, don't get upset." I said, "You don't understand, I'VE GOT THE PUCK RIGHT HERE!"

DON: I love those Rochester goal judges. Back then, anything close, the light went on.

In the opening of the show, I told the audience I remembered one save that Ken made that changed my life. It was 1979, Game 7 of the semifinals between my Bruins and Ken's Canadiens. You all know this story, but I'll tell it anyway.

Harry Sinden, my GM, and I were at war. I knew that if I didn't win the Stanley Cup, which meant beating Ken and the Habs, I would be gone. We met in the semifinals, the third time in a row we met in the playoffs, and it went the distance. Game 7 was on May 10, 1979, at the Forum.

We were playing great and had a 3–1 lead going into the third period. Mark Napier and Guy Lapointe both scored to tie the game at three with time running out. With less than four minutes to go, Rick Middleton beat Ken and we were up 4–3. Then, disaster. I had Donnie Marcotte checking Guy Lafleur. Scotty Bowman was double- and triple-shifting Guy, and Marcotte had orders to stay on the ice as long as Guy was on. Guy came off and Donnie headed to the bench, and our left wingers got confused about who was up and two of them jumped on the ice. We got caught with too many men on the ice.

Scotty put on his power play, which consisted of Lafleur, who had 52 goals and 129 points that year; Steve Shutt, who had 60 goals and 77 points; and Jacques Lemaire, who had 24 goals and 55 points. On defence was Larry Robinson, who scored 61 points that season, and Serge Savard, who had 33 points.

So their power play had a total of 355 points that season. All of them are now in the Hall of Fame. Guy scored with a rocket right along the ice and it just beat Gilles Gilbert, who was playing the game of his life, stopping 47 shots.

In overtime, we came out hard, but Ken made the save of the game. If we had scored, we would have won the game and played the Rangers in the finals. New York would have been a piece of cake and we would have won the Stanley Cup. But Montreal came back down and Yvon Lambert, who scored 66 points that year, scored to win the game.

DON: Do you remember that save on Marcotte?

KEN: I do. I was out to lunch, as you describe. I don't know if you remember that whole series, but that was how I played most of that series. I was on my knees and finished, and fortunately it was Marcotte who had the puck—he didn't hit corners very often.

DON: We stood up on the bench and thought it was in for sure. You were looking away and he had the whole left side. You were right against the post, he dinged it off your shoulder. Oh well, I wouldn't be on TV right now.

Ken didn't go into much detail on what happened, so here's how it went down. In overtime, Terry O'Reilly had the puck behind Montreal's net. Kenny was on his knees, leaning against the right post, looking over his left shoulder, thinking Terry was coming out in front. Donnie Marcotte was on the boards and drifted out in front of the net.

Neither of the Montreal defencemen picked him up. Terry got the puck out to Donnie and he snapped it right away. Kenny was still looking behind the net at Terry, and the puck went off Kenny's shoulder and into the corner. Kenny was so big and filled in so much net—if it was any other goalie, we would have scored.

That's as close as I ever came to winning the Cup. About two inches. If that goal goes in, Harry can't fire me, and I might never have made it to *Hockey Night in Canada.*

So there: it's Ken Dryden's fault I'm on "Coach's Corner."

About 10 years ago, Ken called me up for something and I said, "Ken, you robbed me of a Stanley Cup."

Ken said, "Don, if you won the Cup, you'd be just another run-of-the-mill coach with a Stanley Cup ring and not the king of Saturday night."

That's true, but I'd still like the ring.

KEN DRYDEN ON RETIRING AND SCOTTY

YOU TALK TO SOME HOCKEY "EXPERTS" and they say that the Canadiens in the '70s were so powerful that they would have won with or without Dryden. Not me. They were so tough to play against, especially with what I called the Big Three: Serge Savard, Guy Lapointe and Larry Robinson. One of them was on the ice the whole game. But if you got by *them,* you still had to face Dryden, and he was the difference.

In the 1972–73 season, Montreal had a record of 52–10–16, 120 points, first place, had a goal differential of +145 and won the Stanley Cup. Ken's record was 33–7–13 with a save percentage of .926 and a GAA of 2.26. Not too shabby.

The next year, 1973–74, Ken sat out because he didn't like the contract Sam Pollock offered him. Maybe Sam thought the Canadiens didn't need Ken, either. That year, without Ken, the

Habs finished in second place with a record of 45–24–9 and had a goal differential of +53 and were knocked out of the first round by the Rangers.

Needless to say, Ken was back in the net the next year, and his record was 30–9–16.

If you think about it, Ken really didn't play that long in the NHL. He only played for seven full seasons, and he retired at age 32. That's when most goalies are hitting their prime, yet he had already won just about everything a goalie could win:

* 1971: *Conn Smythe (playoff MVP)*
* 1972: *Calder Trophy (rookie of the year)*
* 1973, '76, '77, '78 and '79: *Vézina Trophy (best goalie)*
* 1971, '73, '76, '77, '78 and '79: *Stanley Cup*

He was at the peak of his career, and he just walked away.

DON: Now, why did you retire? You were still smoking and had Stanley Cups, and I know people like to go when they are up, but you were still in your prime.

KEN: I had pretty much decided two or three years before I retired that I would stop then. It was nothing really more complicated than I knew I would have to stop sometime, and sometime soon. I wanted to stop at a point that would give me time to do something else and to do something else well. If I played that much longer, I would give myself that much less time to do it well, and I wasn't prepared to do that.

I wish I could say that I had had a plan like that to end my career. When I was playing in the AHL, all of us players thought it would last forever. I never thought about retiring or what would happen when hockey ended. I worked construction in the summer, so I

I asked Bob Probert, "Why didn't you ever use tie-downs?"

Dino standing in front of Leafs goalie Félix Potvin during the 1993 playoffs.

Bob Probert and his beautiful wife, Dani.

It always bugged me when Ken Dryden stood like this.
We'd have just scored a goal on him and he'd be like, "Oh well."

Doug Gilmour tying the game at 3–3 late in the third during Game 7 vs. Detroit
in the 1993 playoffs. Leafs went on to win in overtime.

#00 Author George Plimpton just before his 5-minute game vs. Philly.
I think that is Ron Grahame next to him. George left the bench to get interviewed during the game.
While he was gone he missed the biggest brawl in NHL history.

Four-time Stanley Cup winner Gump Worsley in action. Looks like a lot of net to shoot at.

*Paul Henderson
seconds after scoring
"The Goal" in Game 8
of the Canada vs.
Russia '72 series.*

The best Jr. coach in history, a great pool player, and one of my best friends, Brian Kilrea.

My old boss from Hockey Night in Canada *and the* Grapevine *shows, Ralph Mellanby. He and Gerry got the* Grapevine *started. Ralph gave me the greatest advice ever: "Don't turn professional." You can see by "Coach's Corner" I listen to that advice to this very day.*

Blue, not too happy waiting to make her television appearance.

Me and Ron doing a segment for Hockey Night in Canada *during the 2016 NHL finals.*

Me, Kathy Broderick, and Ron in San Jose.
Ron said this picture is jaw dropping.
Another of his puns.

guess I assumed I would go right from the rink to full time on the jackhammer. I didn't have the vision Ken did. I retired on a snap decision.

Ken had a plan for when he was going to retire. Like I said, I never thought my career would end and I didn't have a plan for when I was going to retire. In one game I had the realization that my career was coming to an end.

It was the late '6os and I was one of the Rochester Americans' policemen. One of my jobs was to fight for the team. When you're an enforcer on a team, you have to have courage, you have to have a willingness to protect your teammates, and you have to have toughness. And there is one thing you cannot have: a conscience.

In my prime, I could sucker a guy and not think about it twice. You had to have that mentality if you wanted to have that role on a team. One game, I was racing back for an icing. I touched the puck and let up, and some rookie gave me a slight push after the whistle.

Without hesitating, I dropped my gloves and drilled him in the mouth, knocking out his three front teeth. He lay on the ice, blood pouring out of his mouth. Seeing him in a pool of blood, all of a sudden, I felt a little bad. That had never happened before.

As I headed to the penalty box, I knew if I was going to feel bad about doing something like that, the end of my career was in sight.

* * *

Ken retired because he wanted to pursue other things. He wrote a book, *The Game,* and then had a very successful political career. I always said if all our politicians had Ken's integrity, our country would be a lot better off.

I retired because I didn't get my phone call returned quick enough.

My last year with Rochester was the 1968–69 season. At the start of the season, I was in GM/coach Joe Crozier's office. We were talking about the upcoming season, and his secretary came in and told him that John Smith was on the phone and wanted to ask for a tryout.

Joe told her to tell Smith he was out and he'd call him back. Joe laughed and said to me, "Can you believe that? Calling me, asking for a tryout?"

For some reason, that stuck with me.

Halfway through that season, Joe, who was now coaching Vancouver and owned both the Rochester and Vancouver franchises, decided he wanted me in Vancouver. He talked me into going out there and we won the Western Championship and never lost a game in the playoffs. My contract was up after the season, and I didn't hear from Joe.

I called him a few times, and I couldn't reach him. I was getting mad and kept thinking of that poor guy who called Joe at the start of the season. He laughed at him.

I called him one more time and then said to Rose, "That's it. I'm done." Rose couldn't believe me. I had no real injuries, my back and knees were good, and I could have played a few more years.

Joe called me back a few days later and asked me if I wanted to play in Vancouver or Rochester. I told him I had retired.

That was it. My hockey career was over and my life on the jack-hammer began.

* * *

You've all heard goalies are a bit flaky. I guess you have to be a little flaky to stand in front of pucks going 100 miles an hour. As a coach, you have to handle goalies right, or your team is in trouble. I hear some coaches say that all players should be treated equal. You might be able to do that with forwards and defence, but not the goalies. I'm sure Ken was no exception.

> **DON:** What was your relationship with Scotty? [Of course, I'm talking about Scotty Bowman, Ken's coach in Montreal.

If you don't know that, why are you reading this book?] This is the *Grapevine*; you can tell us. Scotty's a good friend of mine, but be honest.

KEN: We got along well. The way you get along with Scotty is not necessarily the way you get along with somebody else. But we knew each other very well. We understood each other very well. I think we respected each other and I think we were very good for each other. It's a very difficult thing, being a goalie on a team, because either you play or you don't play. You are completely in the coach's hands. The coach can arbitrarily say you're not playing, and if he says you don't play, you're not playing and you don't get near the ice. I trusted Scotty. I thought his judgment was very good and we got along very well.

DON: Did he ever pull you during a game?

KEN: He pulled me once or twice. One time in St. Louis, I let in four goals in the first period. Including a goal from along the boards by Bob Plager with about eight seconds to go.

DON: Now I *know* you were playing bad.

KEN: Another time was in the playoffs.

DON: Did he pull you during the period, or at the end of periods?

KEN: At the end of the period. He never pulled me during a game.

DON: What do you think of a coach that pulls a goalie during the game and not between periods?

KEN: I think it's fine, so long as everybody can understand what's happening—if a coach can understand it in a certain sort of way and the goalie understands it in a sort of way and takes it like a pitcher takes it. Pitchers get taken out of a game all the time. If you're having a bad night, you're having a bad night. Sometimes, you're better off getting taken out, and often you're looking for the hook yourself.

As a coach, you have to be careful when dealing with goalies. If a goalie loses his confidence, it can ruin him. Sometimes, if you pull your goalies too often, they tend to start looking at the bench after every goal. Once that happens, you're done.

The one thing that is tough to see when I go to watch minor hockey is how badly goalies are handled sometimes. There are a lot of horror stories I can tell you, but here are some that stick in my mind.

One year, I was watching the playoffs in the minor midgets in the Greater Toronto Hockey League. It was a great game, and the score was 0–0 halfway through the second period. Both goalies were playing great, making a lot of super saves. The home team got a breakaway and scored a beauty goal. Then the away team's coach pulled the young goalie—after one breakaway goal halfway through a 0–0 game. You could see the goalie was devastated, and he was really never the same. And yes, the away team lost, 4–1.

You have to remember that goalies are a special breed and play a unique position, not only in hockey but in all of sports. Here's some advice from me, coach of the year in the AHL and coach of the year in the NHL—and not only that: I coached kids. I coached the Mississauga Ice Dogs in the Ontario Hockey League and I coached high school hockey in Rochester, New York. The Pittsford Knights and I won the state championship with an 18–0 record, so I have coached kids as well as pros.

You can't treat goalies the same. So all you young coaches, remember: if you are going to pull your goalie, try and wait until the period is over. It's a lot less embarrassing for the kid. If you have to pull him during the middle of a period, then don't pull him right after a goal. Go and tell your backup to get ready, and then change goalies after the next whistle.

Another thing young coaches have to work on is warm-ups. In minor hockey, you have about five minutes to warm up your goalie. I see all these drills, two on ones, and the goalie ends up getting hardly any shots. At some games, I have counted how many shots goalies get in a warm-up. With all the crazy drills and kids missing the net, I've seen goalies face as little as five warm-up shots. Warm-ups are for the goalies, not for the whole team to start doing drills.

I know what you're saying: "If you go to a pro game, you see the players do drills." That's true, but they have 20 minutes to warm up versus five minutes. A lack of good warm-ups is why I see so many first shots go in on a goalie in minor hockey. Then the coach pulls the kid because he let in the first shot, and the main reason for the goal is because the coach didn't give him a good warm-up. And tell your team to keep the shots down! Sometimes, all I hear in the warm-ups is the sound of pucks hitting the glass.

HOW TO SCORE ON KEN AND PLAYING IN BOSTON

I ASKED KEN ABOUT HIS FAMOUS stance. Leaning on the top of his stick with his chin resting on his hands, as if he was looking out over a millpond.

DON: The thing that would get me is that we'd get a goal and I'd say, "OK, we got him rattled." I looked down at you and you were leaning on your stick like you were going to sleep. You had every young goalie in Canada leaning on his stick. Why did you do that?

KEN: I don't know. I don't know even when I started doing it. I have some pictures of me playing in Cornell in that position. I don't remember a time I began it; I don't remember really going into the position. I do remember when others started to notice it and started to comment on it. It was simply a resting position. As tall as I am, if I rested in the normal position—bending over, resting against my pads—it was hard on my back.

DON: Well, it really used to bug me.

It really did. Just once, I would have liked to have seen Ken rattled. But we'd score on him, and like I said, he always looked as cool as a cucumber. Ken was not easy to score on. He was so big and covered so much net. One way was to screen him. It was different back in those days—you stood in front of the net, you got hammered. The refs would say that if you stood in front, then you got what you deserved. I asked Ken who was the best at standing in front of the net.

DON: Who was the toughest guy that ever stood in front of you? That is one of the toughest things for goalies to handle, guys backing into you. Who was it, Gary Dornhoefer or Wayne Cashman?

KEN: Those were the two I was going to mention. But actually, Dornhoefer got me madder than anybody. The thing of it was, he had a terrific routine. He'd always stand just outside the crease, and the crease is so small, there's no room to stand in it anyway, so he was within his rights to stand where he was. The remarkable thing about Gary was, no matter what direction you pushed him—you could push him from behind—he'd fall backwards onto the goalie. So long as the referees saw him being pushed, no matter what direction or where he was being pushed, when he fell on the goalie there was no problem, as far as the referee was concerned.

DON: He'd lay right on ya. And Cash was pretty good.

Gary Dornhoefer played for Philly in the '70s. As Ken said, he made a living out of falling on the goalies. He was a killer in front of the net. In fact, they put up a statue of him in front of the old Spectrum, scoring a big playoff goal against the Minnesota North Stars.

That's about the only way you could score on Ken: sit on him. We thought we'd figured something out late in the 1979 semifinals. I think it was in Game 4, and Brad Park scored on a power-play goal from the point. It wasn't a rocket, he just slid it nice and slow — I mean *really* slow — along the ice. Wayne Cashman was standing in front of the net, screening, and it seemed like Ken lost the puck. Later in that same game, Brad did the same thing and he hit the post. The next game, we scored a very similar goal and Harry Sinden came down after the goal and said that was Ken's weakness.

But we knew it was too late in the series to make a difference.

Make no mistake, when the chips were down, Ken was always there. He might let in the odd bad goal — and what goalie doesn't? — but in OT he looked like a brick wall. Like I said, Ken was a real intimidating goalie. You'd score a goal on him and he'd just lean on his stick, like it was no big deal. It was disheartening at times.

* * *

In hockey, like in most sports, there are certain teams that certain players always play great against. I'm not sure why it is, but it happens.

DON: When you were in Montreal, you used to stone us all the time. I remember we were playing you, and we outshot you 18–3 in the first period, and it was a 1–1 tie. You played great against other teams, but you always seemed to have our number.

KEN: I loved playing against the Bruins. The Bruins were my favourite to play against. It goes back to the 1971 playoffs, but in a sense, it goes back before then, when I played for Cornell University. The best time of the year was when we went to Boston and played against Boston University or Harvard. We'd play the Eastern [College Athletic Conference] championships in Boston Garden and we won all the time. That was the highlight of our year.

DON: There's nothing like the Boston Garden.

KEN: As well as the Forum. Those were my two favourite rinks.

Great, Ken loved playing at the Garden. I would have rather heard him say he hated playing in the Boston Garden.

KEN HELPED MY DECISION TO GO ON TV

As I said, looking back, Ken had a big impact on why I went down the path of television and radio. Ken started on TV before I did, and it got me thinking.

Coaching in the NHL is brutal, and the pressure can become crushing at times. Win or lose, the pressure is always there. When you're winning, you're under pressure to keep winning, and when you're losing, you're under pressure to start winning. I had both of those types of pressure when coaching Boston and then Colorado.

In Boston, even with four first-place finishes, a coach-of-the-year trophy, a winning percentage of over .600 and two trips to the Stanley Cup finals, there was pressure to win. I lived on Rolaids. I had to constantly chew on Rolaids—they were my drug of choice.

One road trip, I forgot to pack my supply. It was in LA, and we got in late to the hotel, and when I unpacked I couldn't find any Rolaids and I panicked. I tore the room apart. I was like Ray Milland in *The Lost Weekend*. I finally found a few loose ones in the bottom of the suitcase, and they held me over till I was able to run down to the hotel lobby and buy a few packs.

In Colorado, it was worse. I knew I was going to have a tough time winning in Colorado. After I was done in Boston, I had two firm offers. One was from Colorado and the other was Atlanta. Then there was one from the Toronto Maple Leafs. I had just shaken hands with the Colorado Rockies' GM Ray Miron to coach the team for three years. I was going to be the highest paid coach in the NHL. That night I got a call from my agent, Alan Eagleson, to say that Leafs owner Harold Ballard had just offered me a longer term and more money per year. I told Eagle that I couldn't take the offer because I had shaken hands.

Alan said, "I'm your agent and I didn't shake any hands. Shake hands, what is this, the Boy Scouts?"

But I turned down Ballard, who I really liked, and stayed with the Rockies. Ray Miron proceeded to knife me in the back after the first exhibition game. Nobody said I was smart. Honest, but dumb.

I remember Rose saying to me, "Don, can you stand losing? You're not going to go to Denver and start winning right away."

I said, "Sure, Rose, no problem."

Turned out it *was* a problem. Not only was I eating more Rolaids, but at night I was grinding my teeth so badly that I woke up Rose. My jaw was hurting in the morning. I went to the team doctor and he told me it was because of the strain I was under. I couldn't stand to lose and it was taking a physical toll on me.

All the things that went right in Boston went wrong in Colorado, and it started with the general managers. In Boston, my GM was Harry Sinden. By the end of my time in Boston, Harry and I were at war and we didn't speak. The final straw, the last time Harry and I talked, was after a game against Montreal.

We were playing in Atlanta the night before we were to play Montreal in Boston. Montreal was playing someone at home the

night before we were to meet. Montreal's GM, Sam Pollock, got
the game in Montreal changed from a night game to an afternoon
game. Then he chartered a flight to Boston right after the game,
and they were in the hotel, watching our game on television. Harry
wouldn't get us a charter after the Atlanta game, and we had to fly
out on a commercial flight the next morning.

We flew into Boston exhausted, but we had a 3–1 lead going
into the third. And then Montreal came back to tie the game late.
I was furious.

I was walking back to my office and a reporter from the *Montreal
Gazette*, the great Red Fisher, was following me.

Red poked me by saying, "Gee, Don, you blew the lead. What
happened?"

I was still in a frenzy and said, "If Harry wasn't so cheap and
chartered us out last night, we would have gotten those two points."

Red followed me into my office, and Harry was already sitting
there. Without missing a beat, Red said to Harry, "Harry, Grapes
said that if you weren't so cheap and chartered a plane for them
last night, they would have won the game."

Harry looked at me and said, "Did you say that?"

I looked at Harry and said, "Yes."

Harry got up and slammed the door.

That was the last time Harry and I spoke to each other. But I
will say this: anything I asked, Harry did. I asked him to draft Stan
Jonathan. He did. I asked him to draft Mike Milbury and he did.
Bring up John Wensink from Rochester and he did.

I remember it as if it happened yesterday. It was 1976 in St. Louis,
and our tough guy, Terry O'Reilly, was injured and a Blues player
by the name of Bob Gassoff was running around all game. He
speared Brad Park and was really hammering some of our players.

After the game, I got on the bus and Harry was sitting by
himself. I asked him to bring up John Wensink from the minors.
I had John in Rochester the year before. John was over six feet
and 200 pounds and was as tough as he looked. He had over

145 minutes in penalties so far that season in Rochester, and nobody fooled with John. But there was one thing: John had a ticket for Binghamton—a team deep in the minors.

Harry said, "No way. We have the leading goal scorer in the AHL and you want me to bring up a guy who's got a bus ticket to Binghamton? No way."

I almost got on my knees and said, "Harry, Terry's out for a while and we need someone to take care of guys like Gassoff. Harry, I never asked you for anything. Please, as a personal favour, bring up Wensink."

Harry didn't want to, but he did. By the way, a year and half later, John had a career season with 28 goals and 106 penalty minutes in Boston.

Harry would do anything, even if it made him look bad, to win.

My GM in Colorado was the opposite. Ray Miron. Ray's priority was to look good in the eyes of the owners. Winning or losing was secondary. It was 1979 and he signed a goalie who played four games for the Rangers the year before I got there, named Hardy Åstrom. Hardy was a nice guy, but he had a tough time with pucks. Which is a problem for goalies.

I asked Ray over and over to get us a goalie. He had signed Hardy for some big dough and Ray didn't want to look bad in the eyes of the owners, so he wouldn't get me another goalie. He was not happy that I started to play a goalie we had in our organization, Bill McKenzie from St. Thomas, Ontario. We started to win some games and Bill had a 9–12 record and a pretty good GAA. But how ironic that, during a game in the Boston Garden (which we won), John Wensink fell into Bill and wrecked his knee. We had to go with Hardy for the rest of the season. I went to war with Miron, trying to get another goalie, and he got the owners on his side and I was done.

I remember when I first met Ray at his house, he gave me a book that was titled *Everything I Know About Hockey*. It was filled with blank pages. Little did I know how true that was.

Of course, we didn't make the playoffs and Ralph Mellanby asked me to do some telecasting on *Hockey Night in Canada*. I loved it. It was fun and there wasn't the pressure to win.

* * *

I thought I was going to get another coaching job the next year, but the phone didn't ring. I quickly realized I had gone to war with two GMs, the NHL was an old boys' club, and I was going to get blackballed. Funny thing was, without a coaching job on the horizon, I stopped grinding my teeth and I didn't need any Rolaids.

That spring, 1981, I was offered the job coaching Team Canada at the World Championship in Sweden. I didn't really want to go, but they said my son, Tim, could come along as a stick boy, so I said OK.

Guess who was going to do the colour for the telecast back to Canada? Ken Dryden.

The pressure ramped up right away. Back on the Rolaids horse I climbed. To say things got a little strange over there would be an understatement. We had a not-bad team, led by Lanny McDonald, Mike Gartner, Dennis Maruk, Ryan Walter and Mike Foligno, to name a few. But we were two men short at the start of the tournament. We were waiting to see who would get knocked out of the playoffs in the first round, and then we'd take the two best players available, so we were going to play one or two games shorthanded.

We thought for sure we were going to get Wayne Gretzky and Paul Coffey. The Oilers were playing the Canadiens in the first round. Montreal had over 100 points that season and the Oilers had less than 80. It was best three out of five, and we were so confident that the Oilers were going to lose that we had already made up Gretzky and Coffey sweaters. And then Edmonton won three straight. So instead of Gretzky and Coffey, we took Guy Lafleur and Larry Robinson, which was OK with me.

I was pacing back and forth before the first game. I took a look out at the crowd, and as I popped another Rolaid in my mouth, I saw Ken Dryden sitting in the television area, ready to do colour. I remember he was looking great, wearing a blue blazer. He didn't have a care in the world. I popped another Rolaid.

Our first game was against the Finns, and we won, 4–3. Our goalie, John Garrett, played great and Mike Gartner scored two goals. So far, so good. The next morning, Guy and Larry arrived. They had flown all night and had jet lag. We played the Netherlands that night and they were full of Canadian players. I was worried that one of the Canadians playing for the Dutch would try and make a name for himself and take a run at Guy. I didn't want them to play but the brass insisted. Guy and Larry dressed and we won, 8–1, but it was a disaster. Somebody gave Guy a suicide pass up the middle and a big defenceman from Canada who was playing for the Dutch just hammered Guy. I thought he was dead. I went nuts on the bench. I called that player every name I could think of.

As I was going nuts, I looked up, and there was Ken, cool as a cucumber, having a good time doing the colour.

The next game was against the Russians (I know it was the Soviet Union back then, but I still called them Russians), and it didn't go well. We lost, 8–2. So after the preliminary round, we were 2–1, and then things started to get a little strange.

John Ferguson was the GM. In the hotel lobby, he saw a Swedish newspaper, and in one of the headlines was his name. He got the paper and had someone translate it. The article said that John had been in a wicked bar brawl the night before. John's face was purple, he was so mad. He had been in his hotel room all night, but somebody said he got into a barroom brawl to end all barroom brawls.

It all got straightened out because we could prove he was in the hotel that night. But still, the Canadian papers reported something about it, and now everybody was saying, "Yeah, sure, John, you were in your room all night."

But it's true. It wasn't John in the fight. It was one of the brass.

Then we had Larry Robinson wanting to be the team jokester. He got some long Q-Tips and put them in his ears, saying, "Look at me, I'm a Martian." Well, when he went to take them out, he accidently pushed one of them deeper into his ear. It snapped off and then punctured his eardrum. He was in agony, and because of the drug policy over there, he couldn't take any painkillers. He didn't miss any games, just a couple of practices.

I remember coming down for breakfast and he was sitting by himself, and you could tell he was hurting. I said, "How's it going, Larry?"

He looked up at me and said, "Grapes, I'm in so much pain, if I had a gun, I'd shoot myself." The players thought that was funnier than him pretending to be a Martian. Hockey players are strange that way.

Then things started to get a little more serious. One of the players on the team was not really liked all that much by the other players. Things got worse as the tournament went on. After Guy and Larry played their first two games, I gave them the day off and they didn't have to practise. Some of the players heard this one player say something bad about Guy, and that was it. The other players ostracized him.

It got so bad that one day, Tim was late getting to the team dinner at the hotel. In our hotel banquet room, there were two tables, enough seating for about 20 players. All the players were eating at the one table and the player they had ostracized was sitting alone at the other.

Tim got his food and sat with the ostracized player, and one of the other players grabbed Tim's plate and said, "You eat with us." So now I had to deal with that. The guy they cast out was a favourite of one of the GMs, so I had to play him, even though the whole team hated him.

So we're getting ready for the medal rounds, and I look up and there's Ken sitting in the stands, laughing and enjoying himself, getting ready for the telecast. All the while, I'm dying a thousand deaths.

We play the Czechs and we don't have a good game—we lose, 7–4. We have an American ref, and I know he's going to kill us. An American or Canadian refereeing a game involving Team Canada in Europe will bend over backwards to prove to the International Ice Hockey Federation that he'll show no favouritism to a Canadian team.

It was not so much the number of penalties he gave us, but he knew when to call a killer.

We were down 4–1 after the first, and we started to rally in the second. Lanny makes it 4–2. Washington's 50-goal scorer, Dennis Maruk, makes it 4–3 and we're on a roll. *Boom!* The ref gives us a penalty. They score their second power-play goal of the game and it's 5–3.

The final score is 7–4 and I'm just in a rage, and I look up and see Ken chatting away about the game, not a care in the world. It pops in my mind: "What am I doing?"

Next game is against the Swedes, and we lose, 3–1. Two days later, we play the Russians. There was no way we could win a medal, but if we beat them, we could stop them from getting gold. Things didn't start off too well. Less than a minute in, Viacheslav Fetisov made it 1–0, but we kept coming. Dennis Maruk and John Ogrodnick scored and we were up 2–1, but if we had gotten some breaks we could have been up by more. Mike Foligno and Guy Lafleur had a two-on-none from our blue line. Guy gave it to Mike at the last minute and Vladlisav Tretiak made a great save. Between periods I said to Mike, "How many goals did you score this year?"

"I forget how many," he said. He knew what was coming.

I told him, "Next time you and Guy have a two-on-none, give it to the 50-goal scorer, would you?" The team laughed.

One of our players had a breakaway—I forget who—and his skate blade broke. We poured 14 shots on Tretiak and he kept them in there. So we were winning 2–1 after the first period.

I looked up into the stands and there was Ken, chatting away on television, having a grand time.

I told the guys between periods to not give the ref any excuse to call a penalty. The ref was from Sweden and was not too bad, but you could feel he was looking to call something. I specifically told the players, "Don't do anything stupid."

But I guess the player who was ostracized by the rest of the team wasn't listening or didn't want to listen. On his first shift, less than two minutes into the second period, he hopped on the ice and tripped the first Russian player who skated by. It looked like he did it on purpose to get a penalty. I couldn't believe it. I wanted to strangle him. It felt like my head was going to explode.

The Russians scored on the power play, and they took off from there. They jumped out to a 4–2 lead before the Martian, Larry Robinson, scored to make it 4–3 at the end of two periods. Even though they outscored us 3–1 that period, it was Tretiak who was keeping them in the game. We outshot them, 18–10, that period.

I looked up in the crowd, and there was Ken, still sitting calmly, chatting about the game on the telecast.

The third period was close, and Mike Gartner scored with 10 minutes left to tie the game at four, and that's how it ended. Dennis Maruk played great, getting two points that game. That was the first game that the Russians didn't win in that tournament, and they went on to go undefeated. That was also the only game the Russians were outshot. We outshot them, 43–40. Both goalies played well, but Tretiak stole them the game.

The total penalties were seven for us and four for them, but there was one thing I couldn't figure out about this Swedish ref. He didn't call a penalty on our defenceman Barry Long. Barry was a six-foot-three, 220-pound defenceman from Red Deer, Alberta, and he played for the Winnipeg Jets that year. Barry was unmerciful with any Russian who stood in front of the net. He was a punching, slashing, spearing, knocking-down buzzsaw in front of the net. The Russians were terrified to even go near the net. I think the ref was afraid to call a penalty on Barry.

I went to him halfway through the game and said, "Barry, take it easy a little."

He said, "Grapes, I can't stand them. I don't want them standing in front of my net." He had a blazing look in his eyes and I just let him be. Barry was our best defenceman in the tournament and a great guy.

After the game, we were ticked off. We played a great game and we tied them, but we should have won. As the players were getting undressed, there came a knock on the dressing-room door. My son, Tim, opened the door, and there stood a Russian player in full uniform with blood pouring out from a cut over his eye, an obvious victim of Barry Long's wrath. He didn't say a word. Tim waited for a few seconds and then slammed the door on the Russian player.

He told the trainer, "There's a Russian at the door and he's bleeding pretty bad." The trainer said, "I'll handle it." He called the team doctor, and the Canadian doctor took the Russian into a small room and stitched him up.

Later, I asked the doctor what was going on. He told me that Russian players wanted the Canadian doctors to stitch them up whenever possible because the Russian doctors tended to leave some wicked scars.

After that, it was kind of a downer. We lost the last two games. The Russians went on to hammer the Swedes, 13–1, next game and ended up winning the gold medal.

We were in the airport, waiting to fly out of Sweden, back to Toronto. John Ferguson never liked to lose, and he was champing on the bit. One of the doctors had an autographed stick. John saw it and marched right over to him.

John asked the doctor, "Whose stick is that?" Fire was coming out of his eyes.

The doctor was proud of this stick and said, "It's Krutov's stick, and all of Team Russia signed it." What happened next was something like the scene out of the movie *Animal House* when John Belushi smashes the guitar against the wall.

After John Ferguson got finished, there were only splinters left of the stick. The doctor didn't say a word.

Like I said, John didn't like to lose.

* * *

After our last game, I looked up at Ken, wearing his lovely dark blue blazer on television. I thought to myself, "What am I doing, knocking my brains out in the trenches? I could be like Ken, doing what he's doing. No pressure, having fun, and I'm not bad on radio and TV."

Watching Ken enjoy himself, I made a decision then and there. I would consider no more offers to coach just any team, and I had a few.

Now, if Montreal or Detroit called, I would have to listen, but I was not going to go to another losing team and get into the same jackpot I did in Colorado.

Television and radio was my goal, and 35 years later, I'm still doing it, so I guess I made the right decision, thanks to Ken.

KEN ON ME

KEN WROTE A GREAT BOOK CALLED *The Game*. Still one of the better hockey books around. I liked what he wrote about me in the book, and I asked him about it. He looked a bit sheepish, and I don't think he wanted to answer me on national TV.

DON: Tell the people what you said about me in your book.

Ken started to laugh.

> **DON:** Go on. I know I'm putting you on the spot. I thought it was pretty good.

> **KEN:** I'm trying to remember, but it goes something like this. With you standing behind the bench, on top of the bench, on top of the boards, gesturing at the referee, the expression on your face, the permanent look on your face, was that of a 10-year-old with a stink bomb behind your back.

The audience roared when Ken told this. I loved that. I've had a lot of articles, good and bad, written about me. One I remember the most was the one Ken wrote for *The Globe and Mail* after Stompin' Tom Connors died.

I left Toronto early and parked across the road from the arena. I stayed in my car to read, and soon began to watch. People walked by me in twos or fives, it seemed—a husband and wife; a family—almost all in blue jeans, almost no one alone. They crossed the road and, the arena not yet opened, joined a line that already extended along the length of the building, ran across its parking lot, and was beginning to snake down a sidewalk on Roger Neilson Way. It was cold; the snow whipped horizontally across the open spaces. The ceremonial service for Stompin' Tom Connors at the Peterborough Memorial Centre was still more than three hours away.

Nearly an hour later, as I walked toward the arena, a woman in her late 50s approached me. She was from Edmonton, she said. She had flown overnight; her brother, who was with her, had picked her up in Toronto. I met two guys, also in their late 50s, from Vancouver. They had done the same and were going back the next day. They could have spent their money going to Mexico, one of them said, but those memories and stories would last only a few weeks. Besides, he said, this would be the last Stompin' Tom concert they'd ever see.

During the concert, when a town name was mentioned, from one darkened part of the arena or another there would be a cheer. That was their town; they had come. Tillsonburg, Sudbury, Huntsville, even Skinners Pond itself. From mines and fields, bars and hockey rinks they had come. More cheers. From love and life gone bad; above all, from a gritty, unabashed pride in Canada. They had all come.

It was, as Stompin' Tom's family and friends wanted, a celebration—of Tom, his life, and Canada.

I had seen this crowd before, in Iqaluit, Whitehorse and Shaunavon, Sask. It was when CBC's Hockey Day in Canada and Don Cherry were there. The excitement was over the top, through the roof, unimaginable. The great Hockey Night in Canada had come to their town. Their kids were being showcased; their stories were being told across the country. They mattered. Former NHL stars were in their midst, wandering their streets and arenas as if they were locals themselves. But it wouldn't have mattered more if the Great One himself had been there. Nothing was really anything until Don Cherry arrived.

The people loved him. They cheered, they whistled. They laughed at his clothes and bluster. They nodded agreement at his lessons and homilies. They burst with pride at anything and everything Canadian he evoked. He is a hugely controversial figure. All those things he says about European players, women, and the French. His "rock 'em sock 'em" message in a time of concussions and change, that intimidates and overwhelms any other HNIC message, that discourages other ways of playing, that allows other countries to advance faster than Canada has. All this may be mostly true. But all this is missing their point.

Don Cherry is about being full out, no holding back. He's about loving, hating; loyalty, friendship, teamship. He's about *heart-on-your-sleeve, tattoo-on-your-backside patriotism. He's about saying, doing—wearing—whatever he wants. He's about noticing the little guy that no one else notices. He's about thumbing his nose at smart-dressing bosses—CBC, NHL. He's the lunch-pail star who doesn't look like a star or talk like a star. He's the star his fans would want to be. And to them he's not just about hockey. He might be all wrong about hockey. It's all this other stuff. That's why they love him. That is their point.*

Tom and Don can be polarizing figures. They are what they are. There is no arm's-length irony about them. They bear-hug everything. Good-bad, black-white, nuance is for the conviction-less. And in their straight-between-the-eyes patriotism, they have come to monopolize so many of the symbols of Canada—the land, hard work, hockey, winter, arenas, bars, the military—leaving little room for those who feel just as strongly but who express their feelings differently. Many have come to resent them for this. In resenting them, they dismiss Tom and Don as simplistic and out of touch. In turn, Tom and Don have seen their critics as smug and soft.

Yet, a few decades ago, when Canadian hockey and Canadian music were being abandoned by many as too rough and unsophisticated, Tom and Don were reminding people about—were in their faces about—an essence that is Canada and Canadian that needs always to be expressed.

Stompin' Tom Connors and Don Cherry met only a few times, not often enough to be friends. But Don was a fan of Tom's; and Tom was a fan of Don's. And Tom's fans—those 5,000 Canadians in that rink in Peterborough—are Don's fans; Don's fans are Tom's fans.

Even to those who think differently, Tom and Don matter.

I thank Ken for the kind words; to be mentioned in the same breath as Stompin' Tom is an honour.

DOUG GILMOUR

Dougie Gilmour waiting for me to get my makeup on, or "gilding the lily,"
as they say. A minute after this photo was taken a waitress came up to me and said,
"Isn't he gorgeous?" and I said, "Dougie isn't bad either."

DOUG "KILLER" GILMOUR

ON AUGUST 30, 1993, WE HAD DOUG GILMOUR on the show. We
started the interview by showing a limited-edition poster Dougie
was selling for the Children's Wish Foundation.

It was a lovely black-and-white drawing of Doug titled *Killer
Blue*—a play on his nickname.

Doug's nickname was "Killer," and he got it from his St. Louis
Blues teammate Brian Sutter. During a game in Doug's rookie year,
a player gave him a cheap shot.

He came off the ice and said, "I'm going to kill that guy!"

Brian, who is as tough as they come, thought it was funny seeing
this little rookie saying he's going to kill somebody.

Brian said, "That's right! Go get him, Killer!"

And the name stuck.

Both of us being from Kingston, Ontario, I knew Doug and his family for a long time. I played baseball against Doug's dad, Don, who was a super first baseman. I remember he had an enormous glove when he played first base.

I knew Doug's brother Davey before I knew Doug. Davey had a tryout with the Rochester Americans in the AHL when I was Rochester's general manager and coach.

Davey was a real fast skater, faster than Dougie, but he wrecked his knee and that ended his career.

DON: Now, I want to know—I'm interested, as if I don't know—where were you born and raised?

DOUG: Kingston, Ontario.

DON: So this show goes down in the States and sports channels and somebody in North Carolina is wondering, "Kingston, Ontario? What's everybody cheering for?" Anyhow, it's a great city—hey, great people and a lot of great hockey players come from Kingston. You and Kirk Muller and Ken Linseman and Wayne Cashman, Bob Murray, Scott Arneil, Rick Smith, and I can go on. How come?

DOUG: I don't know, maybe something in the water.

DON: Maybe something in the beer.

The year Doug was on the show, he had his best season ever with the Toronto Maple Leafs. He scored 32 goals, 127 points in the regular season and 35 points in 21 playoff games. The Leafs went to the third round of the playoffs and got knocked off by Los Angeles.

Doug could have run for mayor of Toronto and won. He and Wendel Clark were the kings of Toronto.

I remember when Dougie walked into the Grapevine restaurant to do the show. He was wearing a white knit turtleneck sweater, his hair was long and black with sort of a mullet, and he was in his prime.

All the waitresses immediately fell in love with him. It's the old story: when he came up to me, I didn't know whether to shake his hand or kiss him.

For all of Doug's success that year and in the years to come, like many players, things didn't start off easy for him. Doug was a star in junior with the Cornwall Royals of the Ontario Hockey League, but he was small and teams didn't want to take a chance on a small guy back in 1982, when he was drafted.

DON: OK, let's start right off the bat. You played for Cornwall, you set a record—68 games, 177 points. Set another record, 55 straight games you got a point in. Right? Not too shabby. All-star, most valuable player and he's drafted 134th. What happened?

DOUG: Well, truthfully, I was picked up seventh round and to St. Louis—but that is good, I think. When you look back on your career, you go over it and say, "Well, nothing was ever easy," and that's what made me work that much harder. So if I was a first-round pick, who knows, I might not be here right now.

DON: Then St. Louis wouldn't even sign you.

DOUG: No, St. Louis wouldn't sign me. I went over to Düsseldorf, West Germany. I had a pen in my hand. I was ready to sign a contract there. They were offering me, I believe it was around $40,000 at that time, with a car and an apartment. I said, I'll take it just to play. Then St. Louis called.

DON: Isn't that something? And then St. Louis wise up and they sign you. Jacques [Demers—the coach of the Blues back then] takes the greatest offensive guy in junior and then makes you into a checker, to check all the stars. It was difficult for you.

DOUG: Yes, it was. Actually, we had a lot of players, we had seven centremen, and six returning centremen that year, and then I came into the picture. Jacques said, "Do you want to play?" I said, "Sure, I want to play."
"Can you check?"
I said, "It doesn't matter. I'll do anything."
And for three years that's exactly what I did.

DON: He makes you a checker and you score 25 goals your rookie season. Not too bad.

It was during the next season that Doug and I started a playoff tradition. Every time I was doing a game that Dougie was playing in, we had to shake hands.

DON: [It was in] Minnesota where we started to shake hands, right?

DOUG: Actually, that's where it all started—that 1986 playoffs where I became more offensive again, they kind of opened the doors. Grapes met me before the game and he said, "Kid, if you want to be on TV back in Kingston, shake my hand— you'll be first star and I'll see you back here after the game." And he was right.

DON: Tell them how many points you got.

DOUG: I think I had two or three.

DON: NO! You had *five* points. You hit the post in the last minute or you would have had six points. I'll tell you a funny story. Dave Hodge [then host of *Hockey Night in Canada*] said, "We've got to end the broadcast early." I said, "You can't go off early. I promised the kid if he scored a goal, we'd get him on *Hockey Night in Canada* for his mom and dad back in Kingston." He got picked the first star and was out there skating around for a star. I ran out into the hall and said, "Dougie, hurry up! Get in here!" Remember you walked right in the studio from the ice?

The tradition continued even when Dougie was traded from St. Louis to Calgary in the 1988–89 season. Any time I was doing a game that Dougie was playing in, we would shake hands before the game. Sometimes it caused a little problem.

DON: I remember Game 6 [of the 1989 Stanley Cup final], and for some reason I was a little late getting to the Forum.

DOUG: I was out in the hallway for about a half hour waiting for Grapes to get here before the game. Terry Crisp [the coach of the Calgary Flames at the time] was all upset at me—I'm not in the dressing room with the rest of the guys and I'm very superstitious and I need that handshake.

And he got it. And guess who scored the Stanley Cup–winning goal that night? Doug Gilmour. For some reason, things between Doug and the Flames organization started to go bad. Doug played two more years in Calgary, scoring 91 and 81 points, but I can never figure out why they started to drift apart.

THE KING OF TORONTO

DON: All right now, the last years in Calgary, things were a little tense. I'm putting it lightly.

DOUG: Well, yes, it was a little tense at times. Again, I really didn't let anything bother me, but [there was] one day where I heard a lot of things said about me behind the scenes and [I knew] it was time for a change. They said my career was going down; I was only going to play another couple of years.

DON: What was it like to hear you were coming to Toronto? Close to your mom and dad in Kingston.

DOUG: We [Calgary Flames] had beaten Montreal in overtime New Year's Eve, 2–1, and I didn't want to leave the building. I was the last one to leave. I had to pack my equipment, grab my sticks and then we had a team party afterwards where I told my teammates I wasn't coming back. I knew at that time. As I get the phone call the next morning [telling me] I was traded, I was jumping for joy. I was supposed to be traded to Toronto and it finally happened. I was very excited.

The years Doug played for Toronto led to the most exciting hockey in Toronto that I can remember.

His first two seasons with the Leafs, he scored 127 and 111 points. The 127 points in the 1992–93 season still stands as the Leafs' highest total points in a single season.

In the playoffs those two years, he was unbelievable, but the 1993 playoff run the Leafs had was one for the books.

Leafs coach Pat Burns played Doug a ton in the 1993 playoffs.

In the first round, they met Detroit, and it might be one of the best series in the history of the Toronto Maple Leafs. The series went to seven games. The seventh game went into overtime and Nikolai Borschevsky scored the winner.

> **DON:** Now, the Detroit series—what a series, best of the playoffs, that was the best series of them all.

> **DOUG:** Yes it was, it was very intense. If Detroit would have beat us, I believe they would have won the Cup whether they were playing Pittsburgh or whoever. I believe they have enough talent there to go on. We were the underdogs; the guys came up big—certain guys were heroes. I can go through the whole team and mention each and every individual. We were all excited.

The Leafs went on to play St. Louis, and they beat the Blues and Curtis Joseph in another great seven-game series. Dougie scored one of the most memorable goals in Leaf history in double over-time in Game 1.

He had the puck behind the net, faked going out to the front of the net one way, and then stopped and came around the other and tucked it home on Cujo.

Dougie was sensational in those playoffs, and he paid the price. It looked like he played almost every shift, blocked shots, played the power play and killed penalties. He lost about 10 pounds, and he was already skin and bones, and he had two beauty black eyes.

Wendel Clark said the rest of the Leafs were sitting around the trainer's room and having a cold one and pizza while Dougie was lying on the trainer's table with a needle in his arm, getting rehy-drated through intravenous.

As great as the series with the Blues was, the next series against the LA Kings was just as good, and it broke the Leafs fans' hearts. In the first game, the Leafs won, but everybody was talking about

Doug cutting into the middle and my good buddy Marty McSorley catching him in the trolley tracks.

Wendel Clark dropped the gloves and they had a great go. The series went back and forth till Game 6 in LA, with the Leafs up, three games to two.

Montreal had made the Stanley Cup final, so all of Canada wanted a Toronto Maple Leafs vs. Montreal Canadiens final.

One of the Toronto newspapers said that Gretzky was playing like he "had a piano on his back." I can just imagine what Pat Burns and Dougie thought when they read that.

Late in the game, off a faceoff, Gretzky high-sticked Dougie and cut him. In those days, if the stick cut you, it was an automatic major penalty. Referee Kerry Fraser didn't call the penalty, and he later called a penalty on the Leafs. Fraser and the two linesmen were the only ones that never saw the high stick. Everyone in the building saw it except those three guys.

Guess who got the winning goal in overtime? Gretzky. To say the Leafs fans were upset is putting it mildly.

Back to Maple Leaf Garden for Game 7. Late in the third, Gretzky got the puck behind the Leafs net and put it out front. It went off a Leafs defenceman and passed goalie Félix Potvin for the winner. Gretzky said it was the greatest game he ever played.

The hopes of a Leafs–Canadiens final were done.

I felt bad for Dougie, Wendel, Pat Burns and the rest of the Leafs. They fought so hard, right to the bitter end.

* * *

A few years after the show aired, Doug was traded to the New Jersey Devils. There was no room for him at centre after the Leafs traded Wendel for Mats Sundin.

He played for a few more teams, retired in 2003 and was selected to the Hockey Hall of Fame in 2011.

Dougie always reminded me of a banty rooster. Even his hair

looked cocky. He never backed down. He was the player I loved to watch the most, after Bobby Orr. He had heart and he reminded me of Bobby because of their will to win.

He was a coach's dream. A checker who could score and would inspire his team with his play.

He is a beauty.

THE SHOW THAT NEVER AIRED

The last season of the *Grapevine* show
shooting in the Mississauga bar.

For the last ten years of the *Grapevine* show, we shot each episode in one of the real Grapevine bars. The audience would come in an hour or so before the show and have dinner and drinks. Most of the guests would have friends or family with them and they would have dinner as well. The one thing we never really worried about was a guest having too many drinks. Only a few guests would have a beer or so before the show, but that was about it.

Until one night.

It was in Hamilton and the guest was a retired player that I had known from way back when. He came in with his girlfriend before the show and had dinner. It looked like he was drinking coffee.

He had a coffee mug and was walking around the bar talking to the audience before the show.

Tim went over the questions with him about twenty minutes before the interview started. All seemed fine.

We sit down to start the interview and things were going great. Five minutes into the interview and he suddenly went from dead sober to dead drunk. He started to slur his words and talk about how much he loved me and hated Harry Sinden, over and over again. I didn't know if he was playing a joke on me or what.

He got drunker and drunker. I didn't know what to do. I looked at my floor director, Tommy Knight, and he just shrugged his shoulders. I asked a few more questions and then threw it to commercial.

Tim, Tommy and I went back into the kitchen of the bar and wondered what might have happened. The guest's girlfriend came back, sober as a judge, and started to give us heck. She was mad at us for making him look bad.

I said, "You're the one that came with him, why did you let him drink?"

We wrapped up the show and the girlfriend took the guest home. Later we found out what happened.

He had a few vodka tonics before the show. Then he went and got a coffee mug. He went to every waitress and asked for a double vodka and poured it into the coffee mug. I think he had something like four double vodkas.

The drinks didn't hit him right away. But being under the hot lights and with the stress of being interviewed in front of the audience, the booze hit him quickly.

Was it ever something to see a guy go from sober to drunk in a few short minutes.

We took the tape of the show and erased it. It was pretty embarrassing and I didn't want to see it on some blooper reel a few years later.

GEORGE PLIMPTON

Famous author and Bruins goalie for five minutes, George Plimpton.

SEAWEED AND THE ODOUR

GEORGE PLIMPTON WAS A WRITER AND author best known for trying his hand at different sports and then writing about his experiences.

He pitched in an exhibition game in Major League Baseball and wrote the book *Out of My League*.

Sparred three rounds with Archie Moore, who was light heavy-weight champion of the world at the time. Moore gave George a pretty good bloody nose.

George was most famous for a book he wrote called *Paper Lion*, about the time he spent at training camp with the Detroit Lions. They made a movie about the book, starring Alan Alda.

Now he wanted to do a book on hockey. George would go on to write *Open Net* about his time with us in training camp.

Two days before the Bruins' 1977 training camp, I got a call from our GM, Harry Sinden, asking if I would mind if Plimpton came to our camp. Now, I knew George from *Paper Lion*, which I had read.

I said, "Sure, why not?"

Harry said, "There are two things: the Flyers and the Canadiens have already turned down his request."

"So I guess we are his third choice, but who cares? Let him come."

Harry said, "Wait a minute. Don't be too fast to agree. Wait till I tell you what he wants to do. He wants to suit up and work out in practice, and get this, he wants to play goal, and he's never been a goalie."

I asked Harry, "Does he know how dangerous this could be? But if he's got the guts, why not, it could be fun."

I didn't realize till later that Harry made him sign a contract with a clause that said, *I further release the Bruins, the National Hockey League . . . with respect to any injuries, suffering, or death which may occur as a result of my participation.*

To give George the full experience of what goalies are like, we roomed him with a real live wire.

> **DON:** Now, tell us about the roommate we gave you when you first arrived at camp.

> **GEORGE:** I believe you wanted to room me with another goalie, so you were kind enough to assign me Jim Pettie. His nickname was Seaweed because of his crazy hair that resembled a mass of seaweed. He reminded me of the actor Gene Wilder. He made a grand entrance, not through the door, but he opened the window of our hotel room, dove in and introduced himself.

> **DON:** I hope your room was on the ground floor.

GEORGE: Luckily.

We all know goalies are a different breed and a little crazy, and Seaweed was a little crazier than the other goalies we had in camp, Gerry Cheevers and Gilles Gilbert.

Seaweed had only played one game for the Bruins up to then. It was in Chicago. Cheevers was hurt and we called up Seaweed from Rochester.

I called a team meeting in a hotel room and kind of went over the game plan for the night. Jim was sitting on the side of the bed, smoking.

I had just about wrapped up and I headed to the door. I stopped and said, "Pettie, you're starting," then left.

The players told me later that Seaweed fell face-first on the floor and asked, "Is he kidding?"

The players laughed and said no, and then he promptly got up, went to the bathroom and got sick. He played that night and we won, 6–3, so at the time he met George he was undefeated in the NHL.

* * *

George and I met before his first time on the ice. George was a big, tall, skinny guy who talked like one of those highly educated intellectuals, with almost an English accent.

I remember a word describing a guy like him: posh. I looked up the word and it means smart, elegant and stylish, and that fit George to a T.

I could not see him fitting into a Boston Bruins training camp, but believe it or not, he did fit in. He was not condescending at all—he was a good guy.

I thought George would know how to skate, but when he stepped on the ice I was surprised to see he could hardly skate, and skating in goalie skates made it worse. He was stiff-legged and skated totally upright.

DON: So tell us about your first day on the ice with us.

GEORGE: My first hurdle was getting prepared to go on the ice. It took me over a half an hour to secure all my equipment. Seaweed, among others, assisted me, much like squires helping a knight preparing for battle. It was secondhand equipment—

DON: Yeah, we wanted to give you stuff that was already broken in.

GEORGE: Indeed, I distinctly remember the odour.

DON: All hockey players and hockey moms know that smell.

DR. HOOK AND BLOOD ON THE ICE

AT THE START, THE PLAYERS KIND of thought the whole thing was a joke. The first time on the ice, he could hardly skate. He couldn't handle the puck. If he fell down, it took forever for him to get up. He looked like an elephant on the ice.

The players were nice to him, but he was still a journalist visiting our world. The only guy who bothered George in practice was one of my best friends on the team, right winger Bobby Schmautz. He got the nickname Dr. Hook for obvious reasons.

He was a little guy, a bit mean, but he wasn't being mean with George; he was just having some fun. It was fun for Schmautzy, but not for George.

Schmautzy would ring the puck over George's head, hitting the glass. The loud *crack* of the puck hitting the glass shook up George.

Schmautzy would also roar in on George and then stop quickly and spray George with snow.

I finally had to step in and say, "OK, Schmautzy, enough." Again, he wasn't doing it to be mean; that's just the kind of thing hockey players do for fun.

GEORGE: As I was taking my first stride on the ice, a loud *crack* rang about my head. A puck had struck the glass near my head.

DON: Yeah, that was Schmautzy welcoming you. You remember Bobby Schmautz.

GEORGE: Gerry Cheevers informed me that his nickname was Dr. Hook and that I should have an eye on him. When I inquired why, Cheevers informed me that Dr. Hook might cut me with his hockey stick. I queried why would he do that, for I was his teammate. Cheevers replied, "What do you think practice is for?"

DON: Remember when Schmautzy lined up pucks at the red line?

GEORGE: The pucks were on their sides, and when Dr. Hook shot them, they acted much like a pitcher's knuckleball. I could barely stop pucks travelling rather slowly along the ice, let alone pucks performing tricks in the air.

DON: Tell us when you became one of the guys.

GEORGE: I believe this is the event you are talking about. I had a hard time with the goalie stick, that I found rather cumbersome at times. I would try to catch the puck with my blocker pad [blocker glove], which had little protection when you turned it over. I took a hard shot to the thumb of the blocker pad and received a laceration. I took off my glove, and to the delight of all the players, they saw that I was bleeding.

I don't think George really knew how much the players admired him for that. The cut was bad enough that he had to go to the hospital—in his equipment—to get some stitches.

He kept playing, never letting on that he was bleeding on the inside of his glove.

From then on, he was one of the boys. We considered him a hockey guy. No more jokes on him, no firing pucks high and scaring him. He was invited to the players "sessions" after practice, and he didn't have to buy his round.

I remember him saying to me, "Grapes, I don't understand it. The players have changed their attitude towards me for some reason."

DON: You bled on the ice. You were one of the boys.

GEORGE: Seaweed was impressed, but said a lost tooth would have been better.

SESSIONS, STORIES OF BOBBY, THE GAME

IT WAS INTERESTING FOR ME TO hear what someone from George's world thought about hockey players.

DON: So George, were the Bruins players what you expected?

GEORGE: No. When I contemplated writing a book about hockey, I was told that hockey players were rather dull and I would have little content for my venture, but the opposite was true. I found hockey players more a "band of brothers" than the other sports teams I had dealt with. I also saw many more books in training camp than the other sports. They all like to play cards . . .

DON: Euchre and cribbage are the main games the players play, and poker, of course. But the players let you in on their sessions after practice.

GEORGE: With beer cans piled this high [George put his hands about three feet off the ground] in the middle of the table. They loved to tell stories during, as you call it, "sessions."

George went on to say in his book *Open Net* that when the conversation turned to Bobby Orr, there was no interruption of the story, no horseplay, and the stories were told with a sense of reverence.

He even said if a waitress came to take orders, she'd wait until the story about Bobby was over, and most times she'd listen in.

* * *

Harry told me that George was to play in net for an exhibition game. Now, this was a different kettle of fish. George was to play in an exhibition game against the Broad Street Bullies, the Philadelphia Flyers.

Of all the teams, the Flyers.

I was a little concerned. We'd played the Flyers in the playoffs the year before and swept them in four games. Every game was a war. One game, the Bruins' Terry "The Tasmanian Devil" O'Reilly and the Flyers' Paul Holmgren got into a beauty of a fight.

Another one of our tough guys, John "Wire" Wensink, was standing on the ice watching when a Flyer came up and pushed him from behind—the hockey code for "Let's go."

John turned around and saw André "Moose" Dupont standing there. Dupont didn't push John, but John thought he did, so they started to go, and Wensink gave it to him pretty good. That was one of many fights that series.

I knew the Flyers were wanting revenge, even if it was an exhibition game. So we decided that George was going to play a five-minute pre-game.

As the players were getting ready for the faceoff, Bobby Schmautz skated up to George, whacked him on the pads and gave him some last-minute advice. "If anybody stands in your crease, take your stick and chop him down." Typical Schmautzy.

George wanted a story like *Paper Lion*, but in that case he had played some football when he was younger and he was on firm ground. Now he was on skates, playing, and in one of the most heated rivalries in all of sports.

DON: Now, tell us about the big game.

GEORGE: The Flyers scored on the first shot on net. I thought, "Oh no, are they going to score on every shot?"

DON: Then came the penalty shot.

GEORGE: The faceoff was in the Flyers end and the players—I believe Mike Milbury was the ringleader—hatched a plan to let a Flyer have a breakaway. Mike threw his stick, which is against the rules, and the Flyers were awarded a penalty shot.

DON: Yes, and Reggie "The Rifle" Leach took the shot. Tell us what happened.

GEORGE: Well, when he skated down the ice, I hoped he would shoot the puck and not try and skate around me. I just hurtled myself at him and he shot the puck and it hit my pad and I made the save. The five minutes was over and I only let in one goal.

DON: Then the fun began.

GEORGE: I was sitting on the bench and I was asked to conduct an interview with executives of *Sports Illustrated* in the Ovation Room, deep inside the bowels of the Spectrum, and while I was away from the action a brawl between the Flyers and Bruins started. I had no idea. It was the biggest disappointment in my literary career.

DON: A real beauty, one of the best.

While George was doing the interview, Wayne Cashman and Paul Holmgren, who had already fought Terry O'Reilly, got into a stick fight in front of Philly's goal. Both were thrown out of the game.

In the hallway, going to the dressing rooms, Wayne and Paul got into it again. In the middle of the game, word came that Cash and Holmgren were fighting again and both benches were empty, but not onto the ice. All the players left to go back to the hall.

I wonder what the fans thought as all the players left the ice and bench in a hurry and ran back into the hall. They would have had no idea that there was a fight going on.

So the biggest brawl in hockey continued with both teams duking it out in a small, confined hall. It was scary.

I was in the middle of it, trying to break it up, and then the police tried. Finally, after a while, things calmed down. The game had to be delayed because all the players dulled their skates from fighting on the cement floor of the hallway.

The game started up again and then Terry O'Reilly got into it with another Flyer and the benches emptied again.

All this while George was talking to *Sports Illustrated*.

What a story it would have made for his book. The game took over three and a half hours to finish. At the end of the game, I think we had five guys on the bench.

* * *

The guys had their special way to say goodbye to George. When he came into the dressing room and heard about the brawl, he was so disappointed.

One of the players said, "George, where were you? We were looking for you. You put us a man down."

George was really hurt, "You should have called me."

All the players laughed. They quieted down when George started to get dressed. Much to George's delight, the players had cut the bottom of his tie off, the toes of his socks were gone and the seat of his underpants was gone.

The players howled when George held up his clothes. More than anything, that showed him that the players accepted him.

As I said at the start, Harry told me that George asked Montreal and the Flyers first. Harry and I never told a soul about that, because if it ever got out to the players that he wanted to go to those two teams—of all the teams in the NHL, those two teams— the players would have had nothing to do with him.

Years later, George told me that missing that brawl was the biggest disappointment in his career.

I told him, "A good thing you didn't get mixed up in it, George. If you fell down, the Flyers would have thought you must have been fighting and fallen. You would have fallen down and a Flyer would have jumped on you and would've started giving it to you good."

"That might have been," said George, "but it would have made a great chapter in my book."

* * *

George's book *Open Net* is a great book written by a guy who, at the start, knew nothing about hockey.

There are some things I liked about his evaluation of me and the Bruins.

When he was doing a story on the powerful Edmonton Oilers, when Gretzky and company were winning all those Cups, the coach told him that the Oilers used videos of the game, and George went on to explain that I used videos as well.

He went on to say that I only showed the good parts of the Bruins' game. If we lost 8–1, I'd show the only goal and all the fights we won. I'd put it to music and the players would love it.

I wanted a morale boost. I found it interesting that the coaches and Gretzky loved to watch only the good things they did.

Wayne sat down and analyzed what he did when he was successful. In his eyes, he wanted to see what he had to do to be the best. Gee, that sounds good. I did it to make the players feel good, and I liked the rock and roll music I used.

I'm not crazy about the way George described me as a small, cheerful man with a cocky manner. I like being cocky; but small?

I liked the way he described the way I got fired from Boston: "That old adage about coaching that if the bus breaks down the thing to do is shoot the bus driver came to pass with the Bruins . . . Don Cherry was fired . . ."

George was a classy guy. I loved having him on the *Grapevine* and the short time he spent as a Bruin.

GUMP WORSLEY

My Springfield teammate, Hall of Famer Gump Worsley.

GUMP

On October 15, 1990, we had Hall of Famer and four-time Stanley Cup winner Lorne "Gump" Worsley on the show. Gump always reminded me of a little elf; he had a dry, deadpan sense of humour.

I first met Gump in the New York training camp. He was with the big club and I was with the minor leaguers. I remember his exchanges with Rangers coach Phil Watson. It was amazing to me how he and the coach would give each other shots, and vicious ones at times.

But I guess if you win the rookie of the year award like Gump did, the coach will put up with it. The next time I met Gump was in 1959–60, when he was sent down from the New York Rangers to Eddie Shore's Springfield Indians in the American Hockey

League. He was being punished. If you acted up or were a smart guy, you got sent to Devil's Island for punishment.

Like I said, Gump had that deadpan sense of humour. When Gump played in New York, he'd always face a lot of shots. One day, a reporter asked, "Gump, which team gives you the most trouble?"

Gump replied, "The New York Rangers."

Not everybody liked his humour, especially Phil Watson. One day, his coach told him, "Worsley, you gotta get in shape. Lose that beer belly!"

Gump said, "Shows what you know! I don't drink beer. This is a whisky belly."

That was one of the things that got him sent down, at age 30, to Shore and the AHL for punishment. In those days, if you were playing in the NHL and either not playing well or acting up, they threatened to send you to Shore.

I remember the day he was sent to Springfield. We were playing in Providence and New York sent him there to meet us.

So we play the game and we hop on the bus and head right back to Springfield. It's a two-hour drive, so we get there around 1 A.M. Gump just stood there by himself with his bags; everybody had left and he had no idea where to go or what to do. He said to me, "What's going on, Grapes?"

I said, "Come back to our place."

We went and had a few pops first and then went to the apartment. Rose and I were living in a small one-bedroom apartment. So we got up the three flights of stairs. We had hardly any furniture, no sofa or anything.

Gump said, "Where am I going to sleep?"

Cindy's crib was out in the hall, and Gump being about five foot six, I said, "Well, sleep in the crib."

So the next morning, I'm sleeping in, I got a hangover, and Rose comes and yells, "Get up, get up! There's a dwarf sleeping in Cindy's crib."

I said, "Don't worry about it. It's only Gump," and we went back to sleep.

* * *

I loved when those NHL guys came down to the minors and got on the bus. They were used to taking a train or a plane, now they had to go 10 hours on a bus.

I remember Gump on the bus, going stir-crazy, walking up and down the aisle. So he was standing right at the front of the bus at around 3 A.M., staring straight ahead, looking at the road going by.

So I went up and whispered in his ear: "Gump, just think of it as a long runway."

Like I said, Gump was always a guy with a deadpan sense of humour.

DON: OK, Gump, what are you doing now?

GUMP: I'm talking to you.

That really cracked up the audience.

DON: Remember when you slept in Cindy's crib?

GUMP: I was tired. Well, maybe a little bit more tired than I thought.

DON: Yeah, you were 30 beers tired.

GUMP: What? Remember, I don't drink beer.

DON: That's right. Phil Watson talked about your beer belly.

GUMP: I told him I don't drink beer, I'm a V.O. person.

DON: That was just before Phil Watson sent you down to Springfield.

GUMP: That was one of the reasons. But I told him I was there [in New York] before he came there and I'd be there long after he was gone.

DON: And you were. Do you remember Shore's practices?

GUMP: I loved them.

DON: Loved them? Why?

GUMP: Because I didn't do anything. Like in most of my practices.

DON: But Shore seemed to love you. Why?

GUMP: Well, he thought I was coming down and was just going to go through the motions and horse around. But I played hard. I wanted to get out of there.

Gump did play hard. He had an 11–3–1 record in the three weeks he played for Shore.

Gump and I had a little ritual before the dropping of the puck of each game. Just before the game started, I would skate up to Gump and say, "Geet?" and Gump would reply, "Ghoo?"

It started out before one game. I said to Gump, "Did you eat?" and Gump said, "Did you?" and it got shortened down.

Don't ask me why we had that stupid conversation, but we must have won the first time we had it, and so superstition took over and we kept doing it.

Then, after his stint in Devil's Island, the Rangers called him back up to New York.

DON: When you went back to the NHL, did you feel sorry for us guys in the minors?

GUMP: I felt sorry for everyone in the minors. I played in the minors a long time. I played in Saskatoon, I played in Vancouver [in the Western Hockey League], I played in Quebec City [in the AHL], I played in Providence, and so I did my time in the minors.

DON: Now, you won rookie of the year [in 1953 with the New York Rangers], and then the next year John Bower takes over your job. What happened?

GUMP: I asked for a $500 raise and they sent me to the minors. Camille Henry wanted a $500 raise and he got sent to the minors too.

DON: Ya know, you talk about great players. Camille, they called him Camille the Eel. Henry was something. He was one of the smoothest players ever.

GUMP: He could score goals. He could put the puck in a letterbox, as we used to say back then. He weighed about 155 pounds soaking wet, but nobody could hit him. One night, we were playing against Detroit and he put four behind Terry Sawchuk, and Terry chased him right down to centre ice. He was going to hammer him.

DON: One of the stories I love is that a big defenceman was trying to get him all night and couldn't. Then, late in the game, he pins Camille against the boards in the corner. He literally picked him up and said, "Now what are you going to do?" Camille looked at him and gave him a big kiss on the lips and the guy dropped him and he skated away.

FROM THE OUTHOUSE TO THE PENTHOUSE

FOR ALL THOSE YEARS THAT GUMP slugged it out in the minors and struggled in New York, the hockey gods ended up smiling on him.

DON: Now, you went from New York to Montreal, from the outhouse to the penthouse.

GUMP: Just about. I spent 13 years in the league, and then I won my first Stanley Cup. I was 35 years old.

DON: Tell us about Toe Blake [the legendary Montreal Canadiens coach]. He was tough, but a great coach.

GUMP: You know, he never yelled at you in front of the other players. He always took you aside and let you have it, but never in front of the other guys.

DON: You played a lot. Any coach pull you?

GUMP: Yep, Toe did in Detroit. I was having a tough night, you know. I've had a lot of those tough nights. I get the hook and I skate to the bench, and I go to throw my stick and my blocker came off and knocked Toe's fedora flying. So we get on the train in Detroit after the game to go back to Montreal. We hit Toronto and they keep us there till three in the morning and then off to Montreal. I'm sitting in the diner car, having breakfast with Jean-Guy Talbot, and I am expecting him to give it to me good. Blake comes by with a picture of me, and Toe said, "You weren't mad in that picture," and kept walking.

DON: The guys loved him.

GUMP: Oh, they'd run through a wall for him. He knew what he was doing. He knew how to handle people, and that's the big thing in coaching.

DON: You were sent down to the Quebec Aces.

GUMP: I got sent down in 1963–64. I pulled my hamstring in Toronto and I was told to go down there for two weeks by the team's vice-president, Ken Reardon. I gave him a dime before I left, but he never called me back. Training camp the next year, I got the call back.

DON: I remember you came to Rochester and you started for Quebec and we pounded you 10–0.

GUMP: You wish.

DON: In 1965, you win the Stanley Cup. Tell us about how it feels to win a Cup. It must have been a thrill.

GUMP: Well, I don't think you can explain it to people. It's just a feeling you get. When you're a kid, you always want to win the Stanley Cup, ya know, go play in the National Hockey League and then go win the Stanley Cup. There is really no way to tell your feelings.

DON: The next year, you had a problem with Montreal.

GUMP: It was 1970. Claude Ruel took over and we didn't see eye to eye. So I walked up to Sammy Pollock and said, "See ya later." Those weren't the exact words I used. He said, "No one quits the Montreal Canadiens." Well, I just did.

DON: What did Claude do to make you want to quit Montreal?

GUMP: Well, you can only take so much. He was on my case all the time. I was never a practice player, never.

DON: Like Gerry Cheevers.

GUMP: Same thing, and Claude knew that. I'd been playing for Montreal for six years like that. He saw me practise. Now he wants to change me at 39 years old. So I went to Minnesota and we made the playoffs and Montreal didn't. Boy, did my wife like that. A reporter from Montreal called her and asked her about it, and boy, did she rip the Canadiens.

DON: I remember one game you played in Boston when you were with Minny. How many shots did you get on you?

GUMP: I had 68 shots against me. With three minutes to go, the Chief, Johnny Bucyk, shot it, I stopped it and then promptly put it in my own net—4–4 the game ended. I go into the dressing room. My tongue is hanging down to the floor. A reporter came up to me and said if I had two more shots, it would have made a great story. I was too tired or I would have whacked him.

NEVER WORE A MASK

IT'S FUNNY TO SEE THE GOALIES today as compared to when Gump played. Look at Tampa Bay's Ben Bishop: he's six foot seven, so on skates he's almost seven feet tall, and he's got big equipment. Gump was five foot six and it looked like he was wearing a spring jacket when he played net. I asked Gump this question 16 years ago, and it is even more relevant today.

DON: Why do you think there are so many goalie injuries in today's game?

GUMP: No respect. Teams have two goalkeepers. When we played, we only had the one goalkeeper. Players would come in and they would stop and pull up. Today, they just keep plowing. If goalies have a mask and a helmet, he's fair game.

DON: You played 24 years pro, 5 leagues and 10 teams and never wore a mask. Well, did you wear a mask?

GUMP: I'm wearing one now.

DON: I know you wouldn't wear your regular face on television. Now, did you have any serious injuries without the mask?

GUMP: I only got hit around the eye once. They just stitch you up and send you right back out there. You know that more goalkeepers have lost their eyes since the masks than before?

DON: How many games did you play in a row?

GUMP: Sixty-eight.

DON: Sixty-eight games in a row?

GUMP: We only had one goalkeeper.

DON: What happened if you got hurt?

GUMP: You went back in.

I knew Gump would be a good interview. I had a great time and so did the audience.

In his career, Gump won the Calder Trophy for rookie of the year in the NHL, won the Vézina Trophy for best goalie two years in a row, won four Stanley Cups, and was voted into the Hall of Fame.

Not bad for a guy who slept in a crib in the hallway when he played for Eddie Shore in the minors.

BOBBY SMITH

Stanley Cup winner Bobby Smith, who now owns the
Halifax Mooseheads in the QMJHL, was traded from
Montreal to Minny 15 minutes before this show started.

WHEN I DID THE SHOWS, I would get prepared for each guest.
Tim and I wrote the questions and then did a little script for the
opening. I would meet with our director, Dave Wilson, before
each show and go over what we were doing and any clips we were
going to run. Each guest got a "Blue Movie" (a play on Blue's
name—we always said she did the clips), which was a highlight
reel of their careers.

I was always very prepared and pretty focused on what I was
going to do and say. But one guest really threw me for a loop.

In 1990, we were still shooting the show at the Don Cherry's
Grapevine bar in Hamilton. One of the guests was Bobby Smith.
In junior hockey, Bobby played for my buddy, coach Brian Kilrea
in Ottawa. Bobby set OHL records in the 1977–78 season with

123 assists and 192 points. Both still stand today. That year, a 17-year-old Wayne Gretzky scored 182 points.

By 1990, Smith had played 12 years in the NHL, won a Stanley Cup in Montreal, was a four-time All-Star selection, and won the rookie-of-the-year trophy in 1979 when he played for the Minnesota North Stars.

So I was ready to do the show with Bobby, and I had all the numbers and teams down pat. We start the show and I say, "Tonight we have Stanley Cup champion with the Montreal Canadiens, Bobby Smith."

We show the "Blue Movie" with Bobby playing in Montreal. Then I introduce him. "Here he is, Montreal Canadien Bobby Smith."

Bobby comes on stage and sits down. Before I say anything, he says, "Don, you got it all wrong. I don't play for Montreal."

I didn't know what to say. I started thinking, "Who am I talking to?" It threw me for a loop and I got totally confused.

* * *

About 15 minutes before the show, the phone had rung in the bar. A waitress answered the phone and then called Tim over. "Do you know a Bob Smith?" she asked. Tim explained that Bobby Smith was the guest on the show. She told Tim the call was for Bob Smith.

Tim took Bobby aside. "You got a phone call." Bobby looked a little shocked, as he said nobody knew he was at the bar. After Bobby took the call, Tim asked if everything was all right. Bobby said it was nothing.

* * *

I said, "I don't understand. What do you mean you don't play for Montreal?"

Bobby laughed and said, "Don, I was traded 15 minutes ago to Minny."

The phone call was Bobby's agent telling him he was traded, and I guess Bobby wanted to play a little trick on me.

For a moment there, I thought I was nuts, but a lot of people think that.

DANNY GALLIVAN

One of the greatest gentlemen and
broadcasters in the world, Danny Gallivan.

THE ORIGINAL COLOUR MAN IN SPORTS

IF YOU LOOK UP *CLASSY* IN the dictionary, you could find the pictures of two men. One is Jean Béliveau, and the other is one of
the greatest sports play-by-play men of all time, Danny Gallivan.
Danny was from Sydney, Nova Scotia, and he started doing the
play-by-play for *Hockey Night in Canada*—in those days on the
radio—in 1952.

During his career, Danny must have called a couple thousand
games, but there was one I remember like it was yesterday. It was
in 1959, and I was in the Devil's Island of hockey: Springfield,
Massachusetts, playing for the Darth Vader of hockey, Eddie Shore.

To say Eddie and I didn't get along would be putting it mildly.
He kept calling me "Madagascar," and I could go on and on about
the things he did to me and all the players in the club. The coach

of the Indians was Pat Egan, and because Shore didn't like me, Pat didn't like me.

One day, we were scrimmaging and Pat was scrimmaging with us. We had full equipment and he had just his street clothes, a leather coat and gloves. He was coming around the net with the puck. I saw he had his head down and I thought, "I might as well give it to him good." He peeked up and saw I was coming full steam right at him. I knew he saw me, and I also knew he was going to jump and elbow me at the last minute and try to hurt me. So just before he jumped at me, I took my stick and cross-checked him right across his shoulder. I cross-checked him so hard, I broke my stick in two. With the coach on the ice and my stick broken in two, I knew there was going to be some kind of payback for what I had done.

I've got to admit, Egan was a tough guy. He played many years in the NHL and was a rock'em sock'em guy. He was hurt, but he wouldn't let on. I knew I would pay for my actions, and I did. The next day after practice, as I was taking my equipment off, he came up to me—I can still see him, wearing a white robe and shuffling along in little slippers—and he handed me an envelope.

He smiled and said, "Here's a little something I'm sure you'll enjoy."

In the envelope, it said I was being sent to Three Rivers, Quebec, in the Eastern Professional League, a lower league than the AHL, which Springfield was in.

* * *

I hope the readers don't mind me telling a quick story about Pat. In 1995, the old Boston Garden was closing. They had a celebration called "The Last Hurrah." They invited all the players and coaches from the past, and of course, I was invited.

Harry Sinden, the GM when I was coaching the Bruins, was bringing me around and introducing me to everybody. I'm not bashful to say I was a pretty big deal in Boston. Coaching the Bruins and Bobby Orr, and now a star on *Hockey Night in Canada*. As we were going around, Harry introduced me to Pat.

A thousand things went through my mind about what to say to Pat, but I chickened out and said, "Yeah, I know Pat."

Pat said nothing, but I could see the hate in his eyes. I could see he was thinking, "How did this asshole ever get to coach the Bruins?" It felt good.

* * *

As I was leaving the rink, I ran into Shore. Not wanting to give Shore any satisfaction, I said, "Thanks, Eddie. How do you get to Three Rivers?"

Now he was mad that I wasn't showing any emotion. "Easy, Madagascar. Go through Vermont, New Hampshire, hit the Canadian border, and turn left."

I asked, "Eddie, why 'Madagascar'?"

He dryly said, "Because that is where I'd send you if I could."

I had to tell Rose that we were going to Quebec. She didn't complain—packed all of our belongings in three small boxes and a couple of suitcases. I can still see her putting a half a bottle of ketchup and mustard in a box because we couldn't afford to throw them away.

We put them in the car with our daughter, Cindy, in the back and headed to parts unknown. It was a five-hour trip, and around 9 P.M. it was pitch black out as we took a ferry across the St. Lawrence River to get to where we were staying in Cap-de-la-Madeleine. Rose and Cindy were asleep. I got out of the car and stood by the door of the captain's wheelhouse. They had the Montreal–Boston game on the radio. I stood outside the wheelhouse, freezing, listening to Danny Gallivan calling the game.

I was in my seventh year of pro hockey. I had been playing in the American Hockey League in Springfield and now I was going to the Three Rivers Lions in the EPHL. My dream of making the

NHL was starting to fade. I still thought that maybe someday Danny Gallivan might be calling my name in an NHL game.

Fast-forward some 20 years later and I'm working for *Hockey Night in Canada*, doing colour with Danny in the Montreal Forum. And they say there is no God. I was as nervous as for any game I played or coached. Danny, always classy, told me to relax and just pretend that it was just the two of us talking.

I told Danny the story of how I had listened to him on that ferry in the middle of the St. Lawrence River, one of the lower points in my life.

"Who was playing?" he asked.

"Boston was in Montreal," I told him.

Danny then asked me, "Who won?" I told him I couldn't remember. He said, "Well, then, I guess I didn't do a very good job if you can't remember who won."

After the first period, Montreal and Detroit were tied at 0–0. Danny asked me what I thought of the game so far. "Well, Danny, I got to tell ya, that was a brutal first period. The only star in this game so far is the Zamboni driver."

Without missing a beat, Danny said, "Yes, Mr. Cherry, that first period was like a hobo's coat. Shabby."

The next day, we both got letters from the CBC, reprimanding us for "knocking the product." It was the first time ever that Danny got a letter being reprimanded, and it had to be with me.

* * *

We interviewed Danny in September of 1989. He was 72 years old and having him on the show was a great thrill for me. I thought I'd start Danny off with a hard question.

DON: So, Danny, how did you get into broadcasting?

DANNY: Before we get started, I want to say what a thrill it is for me to be here with an international talent like yourself. [Danny said it with a straight face. He loved to kid everybody.]

DON: I told you Danny was a great guy.

DANNY: This is leading up to a little anecdote, and you might be a little deflated after this. So hang on.

DON: All right.

DANNY: We went to New York in the spring of '82 to do an Islanders vs. Rangers game. Do you remember that?

DON: Yes, I do.

DANNY: That afternoon, we walked from the Summit Hotel to Madison Square Garden. After the pre-game skate, Don said, "Let's walk back." You know how he loves clothes; it took us three hours to get back. But just outside Madison Square Garden, there is a shirt shop. We went in, and these two fine young men were running the place. Don went over to look at some shirts. Don said to these two men, "I'd like two shirts." Well, these two young men looked at each other, and one pulled out some shirts and showed Don. One of them said, "Hey, aren't you Don Cherry, the guy on *Hockey Night in Canada*, the guy on television?" Don said, "Well, yes I am. Make that five shirts!"

DON: That's true except for one thing; you wanted to walk back, not me. It was 22 blocks back to the hotel. When we got back to the hotel, I went up to my room and collapsed and you went on for a longer stroll. Now, I heard you were a pretty good ballplayer.

DANNY: Well, I thought I was. In '38, I went away to the New York Giants camp in Baton Rouge, Louisiana, and I had a chance to go to Class D ball. I think they were paying $40 a week. So I went back to Sydney, Nova Scotia, and worked in the steel plant and then got a chance to go to college.

DON: How did you get started in broadcasting?

DANNY: I got into broadcasting in the spring of 1943. I was just graduated from college with a BA—what can you do with a BA? Thank goodness a radio station opened. As a matter of fact, they intended to use the radio station to disseminate the educational program that they have there—adult education. And it was supposed to be non-commercial. We were on the air about a week and we found out by sending education signals, that you couldn't live by that alone. So we had to go commercial. We weren't on the basic network of the CBC, which meant that we had to do all the programming. And so the manager said, "Well, we gotta put something on the air, and you're interested in sports. Do the college hockey games, the football games, and the boxing and all that."

DON: So, what is the biggest difference now in broadcasting than when you started?

DANNY: Well, if you're talking about broadcasting as such, let's take it to the major-league level, National Hockey League. I would say the big difference is the entourage, the number of people you have with you. When I started, first of all, you went on the air, say, at eight o'clock and there was no one there to help you. I always used to be a disaster in giving commercial breaks, and I had to do them myself and I missed most of them. But then, after a few years . . . I'll tell you how the colour man started. You'd be interested in this.

In 1957, the Canadiens had wrapped up their series, and I was asked to go down to Boston to do a New York Rangers–Boston Bruins game. And I was up there on the catwalk, a beautiful spot from which to broadcast the game in Boston, and Frank Selke Jr. came along as a producer of some sort. But I was doing the talking, calling the action of the game, and Frank was helping me out by giving the cue for commercials, and there was a wild pileup in front of the net and the puck got caught up in somebody's paraphernalia. We couldn't find it.

I said, "There's no puck!" I said, "Frank," just like that, "Frank, we gotta get the puck." They didn't have buckets of pucks like there is today. I said, "It's rather essential, if we're going to play hockey, to have a puck." And Frank came out with some astute observation and Ted Hough [executive producer of *Hockey Night in Canada* back then] was back in Toronto. And he was listening, and Ted said, "You know, that sounded good—another voice." And from that day on came the colour man, the analyst.

DON: That's why I'm sitting here today—on account of Frank Selke.

DANNY: Well, give him 10 percent of your earnings.

DON: All right, maybe I will. No, I don't think so.

DANNY: Which would be considerable. And one other change—the facilities. Some of the rinks were absolutely atrocious from which to do hockey games. I remember in '53, my first year doing a series between Chicago and Montreal. The Canadiens were down in the series, 3–2. And we broadcasted the game from the organ loft down at the one end of the arena. And it was a big night for Montreal. Dick Irvin [Montreal's coach] decided to bench four of his regulars, he brought up four players from the minors, and one was a guy that was wearing a toque—Jacques Plante—and Jacques came in that night and he shut out Chicago. But I remember the first goal—Geoffrion, I lost him at centre ice, he went into the smoke. I couldn't see the other end of the rink, and the only reason I knew there was a goal: the red light came through the smoke. So the facilities were just gosh-awful.

DANNY GALLIVAN VS. THE ENGLISH PROFESSORS

DANNY CAME UP WITH HOCKEY WORDS and phrases that only sounded great when said by Danny—none better than spin-arama. When he said it, the fans went wild. People would listen to the games just to hear what Danny would come up with next. The hockey world started calling them Gallivanisms. Danny just wouldn't say, "A great save." He'd say something like, "A scintillating save." It sounded so right when Danny said it. If anybody else said something like that, you'd roll your eyes. Danny was an original, that is for sure.

> **DON:** Now, when did you come up with *spinarama* and *cannonading*? Do I say that right?

> **DANNY:** Well, no, you do it well—better than I did. Spinarama . . . I remember in '66–67, that's when the National Hockey League expanded. They were too ambitious with the expansion in 1967, they brought in six teams too many, with the result that the Canadiens were a powerhouse then, as they have been so often. You know that—

DON: Yes, Danny. He keeps bringing that up.

DANNY: I remember in the fall of '67, Minnesota coming up to Montreal for their first game. Their objective was to keep the score down. What happened, they were shooting the puck down the ice in the first period. They just kept icing it. And I remember Toe Blake said after the game that was without doubt the worst hockey game he'd ever seen. So I was having difficulty, I found it boring saying the same thing over and over, and if I felt bored, I'd say to myself— and I'd never say this publicly, but I'd say to myself—how boring it must be for the people at home watching it.

And I remember a couple of weeks later, going to Oakland—the Oakland Golden Seals were to play the Montreal Canadiens. And I walked down the street the afternoon of the game, and in those days everything was "rama"—Bowl-a-rama, everything was "rama." So I remember the first rush was made by Savard [for all you non–hockey fans, Serge Savard was a Hall of Fame defenceman who played for the Habs], and he had that habit of stopping and spinning around. And in my mind, I was thinking that afternoon, if I could work in something, and I called it "spinarama."

Then, when I came back, I looked for a little alliteration and Savard starts with an S, so I called it a Savardian spinarama. It made it sound like a hell of a play, but there was nothing to the play.

And cannonading, that wasn't by design, that was by accident. Canadiens were on the power play down the south end of the Forum, I visualize it as if it were yesterday, and they had Béliveau at centre, Rocket [Richard] at right wing, [Dickie] Moore left wing, [Doug] Harvey on the left point, Boom Boom [Geoffrion] on the right point.

DON: Geez, that's a pretty good power play.

DANNY: Heck of a power play. So anyway, there was a false start, so I had a few extra seconds. You give a broadcaster a few extra seconds, he starts to think something is going to happen. And I visualized Béliveau getting that puck back to Geoffrion, and Geoffrion had a great shot—yes, Boom Boom Geoffrion had the big boom boom shot. And I visualized that coming back, and by golly, didn't Béliveau get it right back on his stick, and I visualized that going off of his stick just like a cannon, and that's what it did. And so I said "cannonading shot," and I knew right away there was no such word and I made a mistake. And I felt badly that night, until four days later, I got a letter from some pseudo–English professor from some college. You should see some of the letters I get from the English department, I'll tell you that. It's unbelievable. One said, "How dare you? There is no such word." Oh, that annoyed me. I wrote back, I said, "How dare you—there is now."

DON: What was the other one I like—*scintillating* or something like that.

DANNY: Something like that. I first used that in a Quebec playoff game. I said that [Dan] Bouchard made a scintillating save. I looked at it on the replay, and the puck wasn't even on the net.

DON: Tell us about Toe Blake. He was one of the few guys you got close to.

DANNY: Toe Blake, I had great admiration for him. I would say the greatest coach that I have ever seen. Would you not agree?

DON: Absolutely.

DANNY: He was a tough, tough loser. I remember when Yvan Cournoyer was brought up from the minors. The fans and the media wanted Cournoyer to play—he was a scorer. Blake said, "No. I'm going to spot him, play the power play, perhaps. The guy can't check." So they play the game at the Forum. Remember Dutchie [Dutchie Van Eden, a regular at the Forum who had a big megaphone and would lead the crowd in chants like "Go Habs, go" and such] used to be at the Forum and lead the fans in the "Charge! Charge! Charge!" chant? He would be up at the first standing-room level, and he had his group with him this night. Montreal was playing Detroit, and they were losing by a goal late in the second period. Dutchie started the chant, "We want Cournoyer. Blake, put Cournoyer in!"

So, less than a minute to go in the second period, Blake puts Cournoyer on. The first time he steps on the ice, the player he's supposed to be checking scores. The period ends. You remember how Blake would have his hat tilted back and he waited till the players would file past him and he would follow into the dressing room? Well, instead of following the team into the dressing room, he went right up to the stands where Dutchie was and grabbed him and almost choked him.

* * *

When we'd be on the road doing a game and we'd go out for a few drinks after, I'd naturally have a beer, and Danny would drink gin and Coke.

In the mid-'80s, we would do the *Hockey Night in Canada* games out of Maple Leaf Gardens. For some reason, the producers would want us down at the Gardens around 3 P.M. for an 8 P.M. game. Now, some of the on-air guys would tape some interviews or something, but most of the time we'd be hanging around the Gardens, and by game time we'd be half asleep.

Danny wouldn't come down that early and had gotten in a lot of trouble because of it. He was smart. He'd say that he'd be wiped out even before the game started, hanging around that long doing nothing. What were they going to do? It was Danny Gallivan—were they going to fire him? I think not.

Danny would go to the Gardens or Forum and watch the warm-up from up high. I can see him now, sharply dressed, hair black, semi curly and slicked back, smoking using a black cigarette holder. He'd be studying the players and their numbers intently. Nobody bothered him, his was in a zone getting ready for the game.

Sometimes he would turn to me during the broadcast and ask me a question. He had an uncanny knack for knowing when teams would score, and he never got caught off guard. Only two things bugged Danny in hockey: icing the puck and that bloody organ in the Forum.

Danny was one of a kind. There is no doubt in my mind that one of the reasons *Hockey Night in Canada* became so popular was because of Foster Hewitt and Danny Gallivan.

As I said at the start, Danny was full of class. I remember going to breakfast with Danny, and he would say to the waitress, "Good morning, and what is your name?" Most of the time, the waitress would recognize Danny and be thrilled to meet him.

If the waitress said her name was Diana, Danny would go on: "Diana, what a beautiful name." He would charm the waitress just as he would charm the Queen of England, and it was not phony. He was a true Canadian gentleman. What an honour to be in the same booth as Danny Gallivan.

PAUL HENDERSON

Paul talking about Team Canada's time in Russia.
It's crazy that Paul's not in the Hockey Hall of Fame. That is his picture behind
me, scoring the Big Goal against Tretiak and the Russians in 1972.

THE '72 SERIES

THE 1972 SERIES BETWEEN CANADA AND Russia is the greatest
series of hockey games of all time. The whole of Canada was
tuned in for that final game. Teachers even had TVs brought into
the classrooms to watch the game.

It was our culture vs. their culture. Going to Russia, we had to
win three out of four games to win the series. We had to play in
their rink—remember, our guys had hardly ever played on the big
international ice back then—they used hand-picked Russian referees, and I could go on.

I still get a thrill hearing Foster Hewitt's call from Game 8:
"Cournoyer has it on that wing. Here's a shot. Henderson made
a wild stab for it and fell. Here's another shot right in front. They
score! Henderson! Henderson has scored for Canada!"

When I agreed to do the *Grapevine* shows, one of the first guests I wanted to interview was Paul Henderson, the hero of the 1972 series.

Everybody remembers him scoring the winning goal in the last game, but Paul scored the last *three* game-winning goals for Canada. He scored the winner in Game 6, a 3–2 win; the winner in Game 7, with less than three minutes to go; and of course the series winner in Game 8, with 34 seconds left.

If Paul wasn't on Team Canada, the Russians would have won the series, but he came through for Canada.

> **DON:** The old story, you played 18 years of pro hockey and you're remembered for the last 10 minutes of one game. Did you ever get tired talking about that goal?

> **PAUL:** No, not at all. Most Canadians I meet for the first time will generally tell me where they were when I scored the goal.

> **DON:** I was in Rochester, coaching the Rochester Americans, and it was my first year and we were kind of struggling. We were practising and the trainer came running onto the bench and yelled, "It's the last two minutes," and we all ran to listen to the radio. It wasn't on television in Rochester, but we could pick it up on a radio station from Toronto. The whole team was sitting in the small dressing room with all our equipment on, nobody was making a sound while we were listening to the game. When you scored, we started jumping around. I said, "OK, no practice today boys." We were so happy.

Like I said, not many people realize that Paul scored all three game-winning goals for Canada in the games played in Russia. Canada had to win all of those games, but the Russians only had to tie one of them to win the series.

In Game 7, the game was tied 3–3 and Paul was the hero again.

    DON: You said that the goal you liked the best was the winner in Game 7.

    PAUL: If I didn't score that goal, the eighth game didn't mean anything. You saw me play—I never beat two defencemen and a goaltender my whole life. I mean, I couldn't do that in practice, but I did beat two defencemen and the goaltender to make the eighth game worthwhile.

Canada won the series with a strong finish, but things didn't start out too good for us. The first game was in the Montreal Forum. Canada scored about 30 seconds into the game. We thought it was going to be a cakewalk.

Then Paul scored to make it 2–0 and then the roof caved in. The Russians went on to score seven goals and Canada lost, 7–3.

    DON: Tell us what the feeling was like in the dressing room that first game.

    PAUL: It was a time for reassessing everything. Of course, they caught us totally by surprise. Two shifts into the game, we knew that it wasn't going to be a cakewalk. They were very composed and a good team and we realized that we had to have a few changes in our game, and there were a few gut checks going on. It was really good for [Bobby] Clarke, [Ron] Ellis and I, for we worked really hard and were in as good a shape as anybody was. So the Russians being so good, we got a lot of ice time.

I asked Paul about Russian goalie Vladislav Tretiak, and Paul was too much of a gentleman to talk about him on air. He told me a story of when he later met Tretiak, and through an interpreter

Paul was complimenting him, saying he was a great goalie and that he had made some terrific saves in the series.

Tretiak answered by saying Paul was lucky to score all those goals and the series-winning goal was lucky.

On Paul's show, we also had the CBC's Brian Williams. He was over there covering the series, and he remembered it clearly.

DON: Brian, you remember that goal. You were over there in Russia.

BRIAN: Paul and I go back a long way. I was over in Russia in 1972, covering the series for CHUM radio. I remembered the blizzard. We arrived in summer loafers and raincoats and it was snowing like crazy. The thing I remember most, though: we had screamed ourselves hoarse and we had all but resigned [ourselves] to the fact that Game 8 was going to be a tie, and you scored, it was amazing. After the game, Jim "Shaky" Hunt, who was covering the series for CKEY radio—if you remember, Paul, you were being interviewed by TV down at the far end of the rink. The rest of the Canadian media wanted to get to you, led by Jim Hunt. Now, there was about eight big Soviet policemen blocking Jim's way. The biggest policeman, about six foot five, said to Jim, "*Nyet*." Jim, as only Shaky could do, said, "What do you mean '*nyet*'?" and knocked the policeman down with a punch. The policeman fell down and was in total shock and Jim walked past him. The remaining police got out of the way and the rest of us passed and interviewed Paul.

HALL OF FAME

PAUL'S IS A GREAT CANADIAN STORY, and I cannot believe he's not in the Hockey Hall of Fame.

Some of the moves the Hall has made have to make you wonder. Take Pat Burns, for instance. Pat won the Stanley Cup as coach of the New Jersey Devils. He won the Jack Adams Trophy for coach of the year three times with three different teams.

He is the only coach in NHL history to win coach of the year three times. Pat won over 500 games and only missed the playoffs three times in his 14 years as an NHL coach.

In 2010, Pat was very sick with cancer, and he said in an interview that he knew his life was coming to an end. Everybody in hockey, and the fans, wanted Pat to get inducted into the Hall of Fame while he was alive. It would have been a fitting tribute to a great guy and a great coach. It was a no-brainer.

When the list of inductees was announced in 2010, he wasn't on the list. I ripped the Hall of Fame on *Hockey Night in Canada* for being such jerks.

Pat died later that year. Then, four years later, they inducted Pat into the Hall of Fame. Did his coaching improve after he died? It makes you wonder.

I can't understand Paul not being in the Hall of Fame, either. He scored the biggest goal for Canada in international hockey. Not only that, but like I said, he scored the last three game-winning goals in that series.

In that Summit Series, Paul played eight games and scored 10 points. Only two players in the whole series scored more: Phil Esposito and Russian Alex Yakushev, and Paul was a plus 6.

Paul played 13 years in the NHL and had four 20-goal seasons and two 30-goal seasons and played in two NHL All-Star Games.

Then Paul went to play in the WHA for five seasons. He had three 20-goal seasons and two 30-goal seasons in that league. He had a good junior career and won the Memorial Cup with the Hamilton Red Wings.

With all that, he's not in the Hall of Fame, but the guy he scored the three game-winning goals against in Russia is in the Hall of Fame; like I said, makes you wonder.

Paul is a born-again Christian and he was the driving force for the Athletes in Action. He helps many who are having a tough time in life.

I hope Paul and the Lord won't mind this story Dennis Hull tells about Paul's winning goal.

Dennis says he was on the ice late in the third period of Game 8 in the series, and he heard Paul yelling from the bench for him to get off the ice. Dennis came to the bench and Paul jumped on and scored the winning goal.

After the game, Paul said to the reporters, "On the bench, God told me to tell you to get off the ice so I could go on and score the winning goal."

The reporters asked Dennis about this and he replied, "That's a lie. Bobby Orr wasn't anywhere near the bench."

Paul now works with his fellow Christians to help people who are having a hard time in life. He had cancer and with the help of the Lord is back at his job speaking the word about his Savior Jesus Christ.

THE END

THE *GRAPEVINE* SHOW WAS A REAL hit amongst sports fans. I really struggled at the start of the show. I had been doing *Hockey Night in Canada*, but when you're doing colour during the games, it's all reaction. When I got into too much trouble, Ralph Mellanby, executive producer of both the *Grapevine* and *Hockey Night in Canada*, put me into something called "Coach's Corner."

I could do that in a breeze, but the *Grapevine* was different. I had to carry the show, and I really believe that, at the start, people tuned in to see me suffer and to see how bad I could be. But all that changed when my son, Tim, took over the show.

He was just a kid then, but he knew how to handle me, as I was still an amateur on TV. When Ralph left *Hockey Night in Canada* to executive produce the Olympic Games, he gave me one piece of advice: "Don't turn professional."

I have to say I took his advice, and when I see a pro like Ron
MacLean remember his lines, I wonder how I lasted on television.

* * *

When the show started back in the 1980s, there were no sports
shows on television, and no channels like Sportsnet or TSN. It
always amazed me how we were never turned down and got great
guests like the heavyweight champion of the world, Smokin' Joe
Frazier; the greatest of them all, Bobby Orr; Hall of Famers Wayne
Gretzky, Gump Worsley, Doug Gilmour, Ken Dryden, Red
Storey, Bobby Baun, Rocket Richard and Gordie Howe; broadcasting great Danny Gallivan; baseball greats like Ron Luciano;
author George Plimpton; and more. We did over 150 shows.

We paid the guests $500 and gave them a VHS copy of the show
for their mom and dad to watch. We were like David Letterman:
everybody wanted to be on the show. But all good things must
come to an end.

We stopped the show when we were riding high. I was taping
three shows a night, sometimes nine shows in three days. We had
to tape as many shows as we could in a short period of time because
we used a mobile truck with a full crew, and it was very expensive.

The mobile truck was like a studio on wheels, and all the
brains—director Dave Wilson and the technicians—ran the show
from it. In the end, it was just too expensive to do the show.

A lot of water has gone under the bridge since we stopped the
show. Gerry Patterson is gone, the Grapevine bar in Hamilton is
gone, and I really miss doing the show.

I will tell you when I knew it was time to end the shows. I
remember it like it was yesterday. I was about to do my ninth show
in three days, and I was exhausted. But the show must go on, and
I was ready and I walked out in front of the audience, the cameras
rolled, and I did my cold opening: "Tonight on the show, I have

one of the greatest hockey players in the world and one of my dearest friends."

And I honestly had no idea who was on the show. I had to turn around and see who it was I was talking about. It was time to go.

* * *

Well, folks, we hope you all enjoyed the book as much as Tim and I enjoyed writing it for you.

All the best,
TIM and DON

EPILOGUE

MACLEAN'S LAST PUN

WE FINISHED THIS BOOK JUST AS the 2016 playoffs ended. Pittsburgh won the cup and we were heading back from San Jose to Toronto. We had to drive to San Francisco, take a plane to Chicago, layover in the airport and then head off to Toronto.

Kathy Broderick is with me and Ron on the trip. She runs "Coach's Corner" and takes care of us—or should I say me, as Ron is quite clever. For instance, when we get to San Francisco and are returning the rental car, Kathy finds us a luggage cart from somewhere and finds out what gate we are leaving from. Not only does she produce "Coach's Corner," she's also like a travel agent.

My biggest enjoyment in the playoffs is going to the morning skates. Somehow Kathy manages to find a coffee and muffin for us as we all sit and watch the team's morning skate. It's my favourite time of the day. After the main team skates the Black Aces come on ice. The Black Aces are the extra players that are with the team and ready to fill in but not playing. They practice every day, hoping to get a chance to get into the lineup. I feel for them, six weeks of just practice and believe it or not some teams do drills with one day left to go in the playoffs. They are teaching the Black Aces new drills and you can see these poor guys are so bored. Instead of doing 3 on 3 scrimmages and having a little fun—and boy do they sweat and work hard on 3 on 3s—they just do drills. You can see the players are just going through the motions during them. It's usually the assistant coaches on the ice with the Black Aces. When I was with the Bruins I would go on the ice after the big team. The Black Aces appreciated the head coach being on the ice with them, showing an interest. We'd work hard and then I would take them out to lunch. I know how the Black Aces feel because a few times I was one of them during my days as a player.

After Kathy would get the coffee and muffins she would show me the stat sheet. Where would we be without her?

So the season is over and we start the long trek back to Toronto. At the San Fran airport, we have to take a twenty-minute train ride, get off, and take some elevators (because of the luggage carts) a few floors up, fight our way to the counter, check our bags and start going through security. Kathy has Nexus and waltzes through, MacLean has pre-check and breezes by and I have to fight my way down the line to get through security. I know I'm going to be body searched, which is always pleasant because my cufflinks and the metal in my braces will set off the metal detector. I really believe this is the lowest form of civilization.

As I'm waiting in the endless line, I see a well-dressed man behind me. I hand him a tray to empty his pockets and he says "thank you." It's nice to know that manners still exist in this chaos. People are pushing and yelling. I line up at the counter and put my shoes, suit coat, watch, wallet, change and anything else I have in my pocket into the tray. Sure enough, the metal detector goes off and I'm pulled to the side, lectured, and patted down, felt all over with a body search. You really have to see some of these guys that do the body search. I think that they must find it funny to body search people who are well dressed.

No matter, when I am through this jungle, Ron and Kathy meet me on the other side. Ron is there, a smug smile on his face, as he gets a kick out of seeing me go through the trials and tribulations of airport security. Ron says, "Well, if you have to be patted down and body searched, San Francisco is the best place to have it done."

We find a place to have a coffee. It's been a long haul; we've been going every other day for over six weeks. So we go and sit down, staring into space.

It's just the start of a fourteen-hour trip. Kathy makes the mistake of telling us that when she was a little girl her mom used to do a lot of sewing, and that her house was broken into and ransacked and they knew the house was broken into when they opened the front door and discovered buttons everywhere. "Oh no," I say to myself. This is a killer opening for MacLean. He always has a pun for people's misfortune. For two months I've been enduring his puns—they are constant, and after a while they wear you down. I now find in retaliation I am as bad as MacLean as we try and top each other's pun.

As Kathy listens on, sure enough Ron starts in:

MACLEAN: Did your mom come undone?

> **DON:** The police thought the case was sewn up but it was full of holes.

MACLEAN: Here I thought you were just a needler.

> **DON:** Quiet you, button up.

MACLEAN: Kidding about this is un-seemly.

DON: Sew what, they couldn't pin it on anyone.

MACLEAN: Well I'll be darned.

DON: We have to go, I am hanging on by a thread.

MACLEAN: OK, let's zip it.

MacLean gets the last word again, he wins. Kathy just sits there drinking her coffee and shaking her head. I think she'll be glad to get rid of both of us for a while.

INDEX

PHOTO CREDITS AND PERMISSIONS

PHOTO INSERTS

Insert 1
Page i (top) © B Bennett via Getty Images
Page iii (top) © B Bennett via Getty Images;
    (bottom) © Hy Peskin via Getty Images
Page iv © Bettmann via Getty Images
Page v (top) © Ray Stubblebine via Getty Images;
    (bottom) © Manny Millan via Getty Images
Page vi © B Bennett via Getty Images
Page vii (top) © Bob Thomas via Getty Images
Page viii © Bob Olsen via Getty Images

Insert 2
Page i (top) © B Miller via Getty Images;
    (bottom) © M Hicks via Getty Images
Page iii (top) © Denis Brodeur via Getty Images;
    (bottom) © David E. Klutho via Getty Images
Page iv (top) © B Bennett via Getty Images;
    (bottom) © Art Shay via Getty Images
Page v © Denis Brodeur via Getty Images

Interior
Page 3 © Dave Sandford via Getty Images

All other photos courtesy of the author.

TEXT PERMISSIONS

"Gretzky now OK with Fighting," by Mike Zeisberger. Material republished with the express permission of canoe.com, a division of Postmedia Network Inc.

"New Ice Age Killing off NHL's Dinosaurs," by Damien Cox. Reprinted with permission – Torstar Syndication Services.

The *Winnipeg Free Press* excerpt dated December 12, 1938, is reprinted with kind permission of the *Winnipeg Free Press*.

"Stompin' Tom and Stompin' Don," by Ken Dryden. Originally published in *The Globe and Mail* as "Why We Stand on Guard for Stompin' Tom and Don Cherry." Reprinted with permission of Ken Dryden.